D1041084

TO THE
CROSS

PROCLAIMING *the* GOSPEL *from*
the UPPER ROOM *to* CALVARY

CHRISTOPHER J. H. WRIGHT

IVP Books

An imprint of InterVarsity Press
Downers Grove, Illinois

InterVarsity Press
P.O. Box 1400, Downers Grove, IL 60515-1426
ivpress.com
email@ivpress.com

©2017 by Christopher J. H. Wright

Published in the United States of America by InterVarsity Press, Downers Grove, Illinois, with permission from Langham Partnership. Published in the United Kingdom as Let the Gospels Preach the Gospels: Sermons Around the Cross.

All rights reserved. No part of this book may be reproduced in any form without written permission from InterVarsity Press.

InterVarsity Press® is the book-publishing division of InterVarsity Christian Fellowship/USA®, a movement of students and faculty active on campus at hundreds of universities, colleges, and schools of nursing in the United States of America, and a member movement of the International Fellowship of Evangelical Students. For information about local and regional activities, visit intervarsity.org.

All Scripture quotations, unless otherwise indicated, are taken from THE HOLY BIBLE, NEW INTERNATIONAL VERSION®, NIV® Copyright © 1973, 1978, 1984, 2011 by Biblica, Inc.™ Used by permission. All rights reserved worldwide.

While any stories in this book are true, some names and identifying information may have been changed to protect the privacy of individuals.

Cover design: David Fassett
Interior design: Dan van Loon
Images: textured paper © Sherron L. Pratt/iStockphoto
country path © Martin McCarthy/iStockphoto
paper texture © antpkr/iStockphoto

ISBN 978-0-8308-4499-9 (print)
ISBN 978-0-8308-9134-4 (digital)

Printed in the United States of America ♾

  *As a member of the Green Press Initiative, InterVarsity Press is committed to protecting the environment and to the responsible use of natural resources. To learn more, visit greenpressinitiative.org.*

Library of Congress Cataloging-in-Publication Data
Names: Wright, Christopher J. H., 1947- author.
Title: To the cross : proclaiming the gospel from the Upper Room to Calvary /
Christopher J.H. Wright.
Description: Downers Grove : InterVarsity Press, 2017. | Includes
bibliographical references.
Identifiers: LCCN 2016046967 (print) | LCCN 2016055482 (ebook) | ISBN
9780830844999 (pbk. : alk. paper) | ISBN 9780830891344 (eBook)
Subjects: LCSH: Jesus Christ--Passion. | Passion narratives
(Gospels)--Criticism, interpretation, etc.
Classification: LCC BT431.3 .W745 2017 (print) | LCC BT431.3 (ebook) | DDC
232.96--dc23
LC record available at https://lccn.loc.gov/2016046967

| **P** | 21 | 20 | 19 | 18 | 17 | 16 | 15 | 14 | 13 | 12 | 11 | 10 | 9 | 8 | 7 | 6 | 5 | 4 | 3 | 2 |
| **Y** | 34 | 33 | 32 | 31 | 30 | 29 | 28 | 27 | 26 | 25 | 24 | 23 | 22 | 21 | 20 | 19 | 18 | 17 |

TO

ALL SOULS CHURCH

CONTENTS

PREFACE

Preaching about the cross of Christ is one of the greatest privileges and responsibilities any preacher can have. It is also, in my experience, the time when preaching itself is at its most fulfilling and most moving, sometimes with tears and joy together. This little book brings together sermons I have preached at All Souls Church, Langham Place, London, over several years at the invitation of two rectors, first Richard Bewes and then Hugh Palmer. As it happened, the texts I was given were spread over all four Gospels, so I had the privilege of seeing how each of the Gospel writers, in his own distinct way, tells the gospel of the cross and the events leading up to it, and especially how they interpreted it through the lens of different Old Testament Scriptures.

The gospel, of course, like the Gospels that tell it, would be incomplete without the resurrection of Christ. The very first "gospel sermon" preached after the first Easter is explicit on this point.

> This man [Jesus of Nazareth] was handed over to you by
> God's deliberate plan and foreknowledge; and you, with the

help of wicked men, put him to death by nailing him to the cross. But God raised him from the dead, freeing him from the agony of death, because it was impossible for death to keep its hold on him. . . .

God has raised this Jesus to life, and we are all witnesses of it. . . .

Therefore let all Israel be assured of this: God has made this Jesus, whom you crucified, both Lord and Messiah. (Acts 2:23-24, 32, 36)

The resurrection of the Messiah Jesus completed and confirmed all that God had accomplished through Christ's death on the cross. It was the proof and vindication of all that Jesus had claimed and taught. It was God's reversal of the verdict of the court that had condemned him to death. It was the beginning and guarantee of the new creation.

So we ought not to preach the cross without preaching the resurrection if we are to be true to the way the apostles preached both. However, although these individual sermons did not extend their focus to the resurrection, they were preached in the season of Easter when sermons by others on the resurrection would quickly follow in the church's calendar.

In offering this little book of sermons at All Souls to the series of Langham Preaching Resources, I am conscious of following very inadequately in the footsteps of John Stott, rector and then rector emeritus at All Souls from 1950 until his death in 2011, and founder of Langham Partnership. Many of his books, and especially his contributions to The Bible Speaks Today series, arose from his own sermons preached there over decades. It is fitting, therefore, to close with a prayer that John Stott had framed and that hung in his own bedroom-study in his London home.

When telling Thy salvation free
Let all-absorbing thoughts of Thee
My heart and soul engross.
And when all hearts are bowed and stirred
Beneath the influence of Thy Word,
Hide me behind Thy cross.

(Words found in the vestries of St. Mary at the Quay, Ipswich,
Hatherleigh Parish Church)

CHAPTER ONE

THE LAST SUPPER

Matthew 26:17-30

While they were eating, Jesus took bread, and when he had given thanks, he broke it and gave it to his disciples, saying, "Take and eat; this is my body."

Then he took a cup, and when he had given thanks, he gave it to them, saying, "Drink from it, all of you. This is my blood of the covenant, which is poured out for many for the forgiveness of sins. I tell you, I will not drink from this fruit of the vine from now on until that day when I drink it new with you in my Father's kingdom." (Mt 26:26-29)

The words that Jesus speaks in this passage must be among the most precious and best-known words for Christians all over the world and down through the centuries. These are the words with which he instituted what we call Holy Communion, the Eucharist, or the Lord's Supper. Let's examine them in the context in which they are set.

Here in Matthew's Gospel, Jesus' words come in the middle of its longest chapter. The second half of Matthew 26 describes the arrest and trial of Jesus. The first half is filled with the growing tensions over the two days immediately before. Look at the sequence of events Matthew 26 sketches rapidly. One after the other, we see:

- scheming for murder (vv. 1-5)

- anointing for burial (vv. 6-13)

- bargaining for betrayal (vv. 14-16)

- preparation for memorial (vv. 17-30)

- prediction of denial (vv. 31-35)

- intense personal struggle (vv. 36-46)

So these words that Jesus speaks about bread and wine are surrounded on the one side by words of *betrayal* and on the other side by words of *denial*. Here we have most beautiful words spoken from the lips of Jesus, words of live-giving self-sacrifice and love, words we have come to repeat so often—and yet they are placed in between words of deceit coming from the mouth of Judas and words of denial and boasting coming from Peter.

That is the dark backdrop, the sin-filled framework, in which we need to see these precious redeeming words of Jesus, because those are still the realities of our world. Those are the kinds of sins that made the death of Jesus necessary. It is because we know the evil of such sins that we know how precious is the event we celebrate whenever we repeat the words of Jesus.

As we examine this passage, first we will set the scene to help us imagine what was actually going on; second, we will think about the significance of that event as the disciples celebrated it; third, we will ponder the significance of the words Jesus spoke; and finally, we will ask what they ought to mean to us today.

SETTING THE SCENE

On the first day of the Festival of Unleavened Bread, the disciples came to Jesus and asked, "Where do you want us to make preparations for you to eat the Passover?"

He replied, "Go into the city to a certain man and tell him, 'The Teacher says: My appointed time is near. I am going to celebrate the Passover with my disciples at your house.'" So the disciples did as Jesus had directed them and prepared the Passover. (Mt 26:17-19)

It was just a day or so before the Passover, just before the Feast of Unleavened Bread that lasted a whole week. And this was the most volatile week in the annual calendar in Jerusalem. Jerusalem itself was always packed at Passover time. And the Romans, the occupying forces, were always at that time on security red alert for the possibility of terrorist activity, which happened regularly every Passover. The Jewish authorities, meanwhile, were trying to squash any perceived threat to the status quo, such as the one that had happened a few days earlier when this prophet from Nazareth, called Jesus, had ridden into Jerusalem on a donkey and been welcomed by cheering crowds waving palm branches (potent symbols of Jewish nationalistic fervor). Jesus was a wanted man. There was a price already on his head, and he was in danger of being arrested whenever they could get an opportunity.

Where was Jesus right now? He was spending the week in Bethany. That was a small village just outside Jerusalem, across the valley and over the other side of the Mount of Olives. Jesus was spending time at the home of his friends, or possibly just camped out on the slopes of the Mount of Olives along with many other pilgrims. As the Passover approached, the disciples were probably beginning to wonder, "Will we be able to keep the feast together with Jesus?"—because there were rules about these things. You were supposed to eat the Passover meal only within the walls of Jerusalem and using a lamb that had been ritually slaughtered in the temple. But how could they go into the city if it was so dangerous for Jesus to be out in public?

Apparently Jesus had got this all well under control. We learn from Mark's Gospel that he had made arrangements in advance. Another friend of his had a house in Jerusalem with an upstairs room that was large enough for Jesus to meet with his twelve disciples. So they arranged to meet there. The disciples would have left for Jerusalem some time in the morning of that day to get things ready so that Jesus could join them in the evening.

Matthew simply tells us, "the disciples ... prepared the Passover" (Mt 26:19). This sounds very simple. At All Nations Christian College, where I was principal for a number of years, we held a Passover meal followed by a celebration of the Lord's Supper for the whole community every Easter. I well remember that it took the folks in the kitchen all day to get the shopping done and get everything ready for the evening celebration. This would have been true for the disciples as well.

Imagine the disciples hurrying around among the crowds in Jerusalem. They had to go and buy the bitter herbs that were needed to reflect the affliction of the Hebrews in Egypt. They had to buy fruit, apples, dates, pomegranates, and nuts, which were all ground together to make a paste that resembled the clay that the Israelites had used for bricks. They needed to clear the whole house of any possible yeast that might be there. And then they would bake some bread made without yeast—an unleavened flat bread. They needed to have water with salt in it, representing the tears that were shed. And there needed to be enough wine for four cups to be shared during the feast. And then, of course, they needed to get the lamb from the temple, slaughter it, and roast it for the evening meal. Then, after all that preparation of the food, the large upstairs room itself had to be prepared. All the food would be laid out in the center of the room on a low table or possibly a mat on the floor, and then cushions would be arranged in a U-shape around the table. People would recline on the floor, propping themselves up on one elbow on the cushions, and eating from the food on the table in the middle. The disciples would have had a hectic day getting all that ready. Passover was a busy time.

CELEBRATING THE MEAL

But what was it all about? What was the significance of this meal? Well, of course, it was the Passover. It was the annual festival of remembrance, celebrating the exodus of the Israelites from Egypt (Ex 1–15). It was the time when the Israelites remembered how God had delivered their ancestors out of slavery, out from under the oppression they had been suffering in Egypt. A few centuries earlier, the family of Jacob/Israel had gone down to Egypt as famine refugees, but as the centuries had passed, they'd become a large immigrant ethnic minority and, as immigrant minorities often are, they were persecuted, oppressed, and put to slave labor. But God saw what was happening and acted to save them.

Celebrating God. In the Passover, then, Israelites celebrated their God. They celebrated what God had done for them all those centuries earlier. They celebrated the character of God.

> The Israelites groaned in their slavery and cried out, and their cry for help because of their slavery went up to God. God heard their groaning and he remembered his covenant with Abraham, with Isaac and with Jacob. So God looked on the Israelites and was concerned about them. (Ex 2:23-25)

The God they were celebrating, then, was the God of compassion, the God of justice who had brought them out from tyranny, and the God of faithfulness to his promise. So, every Passover, the Israelites celebrated the character and action of God. Jesus and his disciples were going to celebrate that, too. They were saying, "This is the God we worship. This is our covenant God. This is the God who made us his people when he rescued us from slavery."

Celebrating the blood of the lamb. Of course there was more. The Passover was the remembrance of one very particular moment in that story, which is recorded in Exodus 12. On the very night of the exodus, God sent the tenth and final plague—the death of the firstborn sons—upon Pharaoh and the whole population of Egypt. But God had warned the Israelites to prepare for this by sacrificing a lamb and then sprinkling some of the blood of that sacrifice on their door frames. When the angel of God came that night he would "pass over" their homes and spare the firstborn sons of the Hebrews. In this way the blood of the sacrificial lamb protected them from death, and when every Israelite family woke up the next morning they knew that their firstborn sons were alive because the lamb had been slain in their place. It was the sacrifice of the lamb that had delivered them from death. They were spared from the wrath of God by the blood of the Passover lamb.

This was the Feast of the Passover that they celebrated year after year to remember the exodus and to remember the Passover lamb.

Celebrating with hope for the future. They naturally celebrated it with great *joy*, because it was a time of thanking God for his deliverance. But they also celebrated it with great *longing*. Down through the centuries, even while they were in their own land, the Israelites felt that somehow they were still in captivity. It felt as if the exile had never ended—as if they were still under the heel of their oppressors, as indeed they now were under the Romans. They felt as if they were still experiencing God's judgment upon them for their sin. And so, every time they celebrated the Passover, they longed that God would once again come to their rescue. They longed for a new "exodus" bringing them freedom and forgiveness.

So the Passover feast both *looked back* to what God had done in their history, and *looked forward* with hope and expectation to what God would do when God truly became king.

That is the event, and that is what Jesus and his disciples were preparing to celebrate—the foundation event of their nation, and the future longing of their hearts.

HEARING THE WORDS OF JESUS

In the midst of all this, while the meal was in full swing, we read in Matthew 26 several words that Jesus spoke. First of all, there are words about his betrayer in verses 20-25. Second, there are the words of Jesus about his body and blood in verses 26-28. Third, and very surprisingly, in verse 29 there's the word about the banquet to come in the future. Let's think about each of these in turn.

Words about his betrayer (Mt 26:20-25). Jesus addresses his disciples:

When evening came, Jesus was reclining at the table with the Twelve. And while they were eating, he said, "Truly I tell you, one of you will betray me."

They were very sad and began to say to him one after the other, "Surely you don't mean me, Lord?"

Jesus replied, "The one who has dipped his hand into the bowl with me will betray me. The Son of Man will go just as it is written about him. But woe to that man who betrays the Son of Man! It would be better for him if he had not been born."

Then Judas, the one who would betray him, said, "Surely you don't mean me, Rabbi?"

Jesus answered, "You have said so."

The time has come. There they are, reclining around the central food table. The meal's getting underway, there's a general buzz of conversation, and suddenly Jesus says these shocking words: "One of you fellows is going to betray me. Actually, friends, there's a traitor in our midst."

Can you imagine the shock and the sudden hush as it sinks in: "*What* did he just say?" They were stunned with disbelief. Then they all began to wonder and protest, "Lord, you don't mean me? It couldn't possibly be me, Lord!"

I don't think Jesus' reply in verse 23 is quite as the NIV has translated it—"*The* one who has dipped his hand into the bowl"—because *all* of them would have been doing that by this time. That's the way they ate the Passover around the communal table, "all hands on deck," as it were. What Jesus means is, "Someone who is here eating with us, someone who is sharing this sacred covenant meal together with us, dipping his hand in the food with us, *one of us right here,* my friends, is going to betray me." Imagine the shock!

Then in verse 24 Jesus comments on the profound mystery of what is happening at that moment; he says, "The Son of Man [he means himself] will go just as it is written about him." In other words, his death would be just as God had always planned it. "But woe to that man who betrays the Son of Man! It would be better for him if he had not been born." In other words, Jesus' death would be according to the will and purpose of God, but the one who would betray him would bear his own personal moral responsibility for what he did.

But the next verse, verse 25, shows us that Judas was not a puppet on a string, being dangled and manipulated by God. Judas, along with all the other disciples, also says to Jesus, "Rabbi, it isn't me, is it?" This is the man who already has thirty pieces of silver stashed away somewhere on his person, because he's already agreed to betray Jesus to the authorities. There was a price on Jesus' head, and Judas has already taken the money. Jesus has already been "sold," as far as Judas is concerned. But still he puts on a bold front before Jesus. And Jesus says to him, "You said it. Those are your words, out of your own mouth."

When we combine what Matthew records here with what John tells us about this moment in John 13:21-30, I think it is clear that this was part of a private conversation between Jesus and Judas on the one side, and John on the other. Almost certainly, it seems to me, these words were private between the three of them. They were spoken close to the ears of both men. But can you see what this means? We need to remember the way the supper was arranged, and keep right out of our minds the famous painting of the Last Supper by Leonardo da Vinci.

Jesus was the host at this meal. So he would have been reclining in the center of the group, at the top of the U shape. And on one side, to his right, was John, leaning close to his chest. That was the first place of honor. But who was on the other side? The fact is that it was Judas on his left. On the right hand, John; on his left side, Judas. Right and left were the places of greatest honor next to the host. In those days, that was where you wanted to be at any banquet or feast. People would argue about who was going to be on the right and left hands of the host.

So it seems from the conversation as John records it that Jesus was showing his love for Judas by giving him the honored position by his side at this last supper, offering him, even then, the opportunity to change. Jesus was telling Judas clearly that he, Jesus, knew what was about to happen, that he knew what was in Judas' heart. Yet, even at this point, Judas refused to change his mind. He refused the honor and the opportunity, hardened his heart, and went out to do what he had already decided to do. Almost certainly the other disciples did not hear the exchange between Jesus and Judas, or they would have tried to stop him. The whole idea that there was a traitor in their midst was too much to take in, and they were still assuming the best about Judas, even as he went off to arrange the betrayal of his Lord (Jn 13:28-30).

Words about his body and blood (Mt 26:26-28). After that, the meal proceeds, doubtless with a lot of puzzled conversation around the side cushions. Then, in verses 26-28, we have Jesus' words about his body and his blood. This brings even more shocks.

> While they were eating, Jesus took bread, and when he had given thanks, he broke it and gave it to his disciples, saying, "Take and eat; this is my body."
>
> Then he took a cup, and when he had given thanks, he gave it to them, saying, "Drink from it, all of you. This is my blood of the covenant, which is poured out for many for the forgiveness of sins." (Mt 26:26-28)

We need to understand that this was a traditional meal. The Passover had a whole liturgy of words that were said and actions that were done. And at one particular point the host would break the unleavened bread and immediately pronounce a blessing or a thanksgiving: "Blessed art thou, O Lord our God, King of the Universe, who bringest forth bread from the earth." That's what Jesus would have said when Matthew tells us, "when he had given thanks" (Mt 26:26). After that, the host would normally have gone on to say, "This is the bread of affliction that our fathers ate." In other words: this bread represents our suffering in slavery in Egypt all those centuries ago.

But Jesus breaks the bread, gives thanks, and then says something very different and shocking. He says, "Take and eat; this is my body" (Mt 26:26) (and Luke and Paul add that Jesus also says, "which is given for you" [Lk 22:19; 1 Cor 11:24]). This unmistakably means that Jesus knew he was going to be killed. He knew that his own body would be given up in sacrifice, that it would be broken just as the bread was being broken. And he is telling his disciples that in eating that bread they would be sharing in the benefit of Jesus' sacrifice, just as the Israelites benefited from the sacrifice of the Passover lamb and remembered that every time they ate the Passover together.

Jesus is saying, "This bread is *me*. I am the broken bread. I am the new Passover. I am the new exodus. I am the deliverance you long for. But it's going to happen because my body will be given in death as a sacrifice for you. For your redemption, I give my life."

The meal continues as they try to absorb that. And then, probably as the meal was coming to an end: "Then he took a cup, and when he had given thanks, he gave it to them, saying, 'Drink from it, all of you. This is my blood of the covenant, which is poured out for many for the forgiveness of sins'" (Mt 26:27-28).

There were (and still are) four cups of wine during the celebration of Passover. They are said to represent four of the promises God had made to the Israelites in Exodus 6:6-7: "I will bring you out from under the yoke of the Egyptians. I will free you from being slaves to them, and I will redeem you with an outstretched arm and with mighty acts of judgment. I will take you as my own people, and I will be your God."

The third cup was probably the one that Jesus took at this point; it corresponded with the promise, "I will redeem you." Along with this cup, they normally recited the traditional grace after a meal. Once again, Jesus took the normal Passover liturgy and first of all said what was expected. He gave thanks with the words, "Blessed art thou, O Lord our God, King of the Universe, who givest us the fruit of the vine." He would then pass the cup around for the disciples to drink. But this time Jesus says, "This is my blood of the covenant, which is poured out for many for the forgiveness of sins" (Mt 26:28).

These words are very familiar to us because we have heard them so often. If we're Christian believers and regularly attend church, we have heard these words hundreds of times in a Communion service. But try to imagine this very first time, in that upstairs secret room, with these men reclining around this somber Passover meal, when Jesus speaks these startling, shocking words. Once again, as with the broken bread referring to his body, the word *blood* undoubtedly pointed to a violent death.

We need to see that in these three phrases Jesus is bringing together echoes of three Scriptures.

- my blood of the covenant
- poured out for many
- for the forgiveness of sins

Jesus was trying to help his disciples (and us) understand the significance of what was about to happen only a few hours later. We need to see that event, the crucifixion, in the light of the three Scriptures Jesus quotes.

First of all, *the blood of the covenant.* That phrase comes from Exodus 24:1-11, specifically verses 6-11. This is the story of how, after the Israelites had come out of Egypt after the exodus, they came to Mount Sinai and God made a covenant with them there. That covenant involved a sacrifice. Moses took half of the blood of that sacrifice and sprinkled it on the altar (representing God, as one party in the covenant). Then he took the Book of the Covenant and read it to the people, and they responded, "We will do everything the LORD has said; we will obey" (Ex 24:7). Then Moses took the other half of the blood of the sacrifice and sprinkled it on the people and said, "This is the blood of the covenant [exactly the words that Jesus said] that the LORD has made with you in accordance with all these words" (Ex 24:8). And then Moses and Aaron and the elders of the people went up the mountain of Sinai. And we read the surprising words that they saw the God of Israel, and they ate and drank in the presence of God.

Can you see in that story in Exodus 24 the combination of sacrifice, blood, covenant, and a meal in the presence of God? And Jesus says: that's what this is. That original covenant sacrifice with its blood had sealed the relationship between God and his people Israel after the exodus. And Jesus is saying, "This is my blood of the covenant poured out in sacrifice to seal the relationship between you and me and God together. You twelve, you disciples of the Messiah, you and all who will join you through faith in me—you will be mine forever in the bonds of love in the new covenant because I have redeemed you and you are mine. This is the blood of the covenant."

Second, Jesus says this blood of the covenant is *poured out for many*. That phrase comes from Isaiah 53, one of the most famous chapters in the Old Testament. It speaks about the servant of the Lord who Isaiah said would come, and who would suffer and die, not for his own sins, but for ours. Isaiah 53 is where we're told that he, the servant of the Lord, was pierced for our transgressions, he was crushed for our iniquities, and the Lord laid upon him the iniquity of us all. But later in the chapter, God says he will vindicate and glorify his servant. Why? Look at verse 12:

> Because he poured out his life unto death,
>   and was numbered with the transgressors.
> For he bore the sin of many,
>   and made intercession for the transgressors. (Is 53:12)

That's what Jesus is referring to. "This is my blood … poured out in death for *many*. I will give my life as the obedient servant of God in order that through my death I will bear the sin of many, many others."

And third, this blood of the covenant is poured out for many *for the forgiveness of sins*. This time Jesus almost certainly has in mind Jeremiah 31:31-34. In that passage, God promises through Jeremiah that there will be a new covenant. The NIV footnote for Matthew 26:28 states that some of the manuscripts of Matthew's Gospel, along with Luke 22:20 and 1 Corinthians 11:25 (the earliest account of the Last Supper), record that Jesus did say, "This is the blood of the *new* covenant."

Read Jeremiah 31:31-34 and you will see that it is a promise made up of several major ingredients. But the bottom line, the climax, the final great promise that God makes in this new covenant, is this: "I will forgive their wickedness and will remember their sins no more" (Jer 31:34). That is what the Israelites of Jesus' day longed for: that God would forgive their sins, bring their perceived exile to an end, and bring them back into fellowship with himself. And Jesus says, "This will happen. The new covenant is happening now. But it will happen through my death, because my blood will be poured out to bring about that forgiveness."

So you see, by this wonderful combination of Scriptures, these echoes of biblical texts that Jesus and his disciples knew so well, Jesus was explaining to his disciples the meaning of what was about to happen before the sun would set the very next day. Jesus would be slain, his body would be broken, and his blood would be shed. But now the disciples know that, according to Jesus, it would not be just some terrible accident or tragedy. Rather, it would be a sacrifice through which the benefits of the exodus, the Passover, and the new covenant would all come to fulfilment. Through the blood of Christ, they would know that they would be saved from death and given life, that they would be redeemed from slavery and sin, that their sins would be forgiven, and that they would be brought into a new covenant relationship with God in the bonds of God's love. That's the wonderful extent and scope of what Jesus means when he uses these words drawn from the Scriptures.

Words about the banquet to come (Mt 26:29). We've heard the words of Jesus about his betrayer, and about his own body and blood. But he hasn't quite finished. In verse 29 Jesus adds, "I will not drink from this fruit of the vine from now on until that day when I drink it new with you in my Father's kingdom."

Traditionally in the Passover feast, as we've seen, there are four cups, and the fourth cup is linked to the promise at the end of Exodus 6:7, where God said, "I will take you as my own people, and I will be your God." This indicates the intimate, personal relationship between God and his people. And in the Old Testament that was sometimes pictured as a banquet; a future banquet in which God would feast with his people in peace, joy, and blessing. That is what some Scriptures prophesied.

So what seems to have happened at this point in the evening is that Jesus declined to drink that fourth cup. Instead, he said, "Don't worry, it will keep. It will keep until the day when we will be reunited. Tomorrow I will leave you in death. But the day will come when we will be together again in the kingdom of my Father—a day when the new exodus will have truly happened, a day when there will be an end to all oppression, suffering, tears, death, and pain. Let's look forward to that!" That is what is to come. That is God's future, because of what would happen in those next three days.

And so, in the midst of all those difficult words preparing his sorrowful disciples for his broken, bloody death, Jesus is pointing them forward, as the Passover always pointed forward, to that glorious, joyful day when he would meet them again in glory at the heavenly banquet of the Messiah.

I belong to a small reading group. We read all kinds of novels and books, mostly secular ones, seeking to understand our culture and how we can relate the gospel to the world reflected in today's literature. Some of the books we read are pretty dark and gloomy stories of murder, deceit, betrayal, and other evils. We often ask ourselves when we're discussing these books, "Is there a redemptive moment in this book? Is there a word or action or turn of events that gives any degree of hope within this story? Does the author point toward any kind of 'happy ending' even if the story never gets to it?"

Here toward the end of the gospel story we have a narrative of betrayal, deceit, denial, desertion, and rejection. Those are the dark and evil realities of this chapter, as we have seen. But yes, there is a redemptive moment. And that redemptive moment is not just when Jesus speaks about an ultimately happy ending at the banquet of God's kingdom in verse 29. No, the truly redemptive moment in this narrative is actually the one thing that everybody in that room, including Jesus himself, feared most: the fact that, before the sun went down the next day, his body would be broken in death and his blood would be poured out as a sacrifice. That would be the redemption of the whole story—not just the story in the Gospels, but the whole story of humanity and creation itself. The cross and resurrection of Jesus is the redemptive moment of all of history.

SEEING THE SIGNIFICANCE

So what does all this mean, then? And especially: What does it mean for us as we come regularly to Holy Communion and hear these words of Jesus again and again? For if we belong to Jesus, we belong to the people of the new covenant. We share in the story and identity of Israel of the Old Testament, through faith in the

Messiah Jesus. We are, as Paul very clearly told the Galatians, the spiritual seed of Abraham (Gal 3:7-9, 26-29). So as we celebrate the Lord's Supper, or Eucharist (or whatever it is called at your church), we are celebrating the same great truths as Old Testament Israel did, only now made even more wonderful in the light of the cross and resurrection of Jesus.

The exodus was the most important moment in the history of Old Testament Israel. If it had not happened, the people would have stayed in slavery. If the Passover lamb had not been slain, they would have known devastating death and grief. If the blood of the covenant had not sealed their relationship with God, they would have been no people at all, without hope and without God just like the rest of the world.

But it *did* happen! And because it happened . . . they were a free people. They were alive and not dead. They knew they were God's covenant people with God's presence in their midst. And that's why they kept the feast.

And so it is for us. *The cross and resurrection of our Lord Jesus Christ together* constitute the most important event, not just in the New Testament, but in the whole history of the universe, which will be redeemed and reconciled to God because Jesus died and rose again.

If it had not happened, we would still be in bondage to sin. If it had not happened, we would still be spiritually dead. If it had not happened, we would be separated from God forever.

But it *did* happen! Praise God! And because it happened . . . we have been brought out of slavery to sin. We who were dead in trespasses and sins have been made alive in Christ. We have become citizens of God's people, members of God's people, and the place of God's dwelling (Eph 2:19-22). That is why we keep the feast. That is why we celebrate the Lord's Supper together with grateful hearts and with changed lives.

But there's one last detail that we must not miss. In verse 30 Matthew tells us, as do the other Gospels, that at the end of the supper, "When they had sung a hymn, they went out to the Mount of Olives" (Mt 26:30). What were they singing as they went? Well, almost certainly they were singing that traditional group of psalms from the book of Psalms that are known as the Great Hallel. The Great Hallel comprises Psalms 113–118, but it was usually the last few, Psalms 115–118, that were sung at the very end of the Passover meal at the time of Jesus (and still today whenever Jews celebrate Passover).

Read Psalms 115, 116, 117, and 118, imagining yourself as Jesus singing them. Picture Jesus, leading his disciples, verse by verse, in singing these psalms together as they finished that last supper. Think of the words of those psalms filling their minds as they left that secret upstairs room, as they made their way back through the darkened streets of Jerusalem, down the valley, up the wooded slopes of the Mount of Olives, and toward the garden that was called Gethsemane.

These were the words that were in the mind, the voice, of Jesus himself in those final hours before his betrayal, trial, and death. Jesus would have sung Psalm 116:

> I love the LORD, for he heard my voice;
>   he heard my cry for mercy.
> Because he turned his ear to me,
>   I will call on him as long as I live.
> The cords of death entangled me,
>   the anguish of the grave came over me;
>   I was overcome by distress and sorrow.
> Then I called on the name of the LORD:
>   "LORD, save me!" (Ps 116:1-4)

Were these words filling his mind in the agony of his prayer to his Father in Gethsemane?

> For you, LORD, have delivered me from death,
>   my eyes from tears,
>   my feet from stumbling,
> that I may walk before the LORD
>   in the land of the living.
> I trusted in the LORD when I said,
>   "I am greatly afflicted" . . .
>
> I will fulfill my vows to the LORD
>   in the presence of all his people.
> Precious in the sight of the LORD
>   is the death of his faithful servants.
> Truly I am your servant, LORD;
>   I serve you just as my mother did. (Ps 116:8-10, 14-16)

And in Psalm 118 Jesus would have sung these words:

> I will not die but live,
>   and will proclaim what the LORD has done.
> The LORD has chastened me severely,
>   but he has not given me over to death. (Ps 118:17-18)

But the Lord *did* give Jesus over to death. Indeed, Jesus gave himself over to a death that would be no less terrifying and agonizing because he knew that God would raise him from the dead. And at the climax of Psalm 118, Jesus would have sung these words with his disciples: "*You are my God*, and I will praise you; *you are my God*, and I will exalt you" (Ps 118:28, emphasis mine).

But twelve hours later, Jesus cried out these terrible words with their unmistakable echo: "My God, my God, *why have you forsaken me?*" (Ps 22:1, emphasis mine). Why indeed? Because Jesus was bearing the sin of the world, your sin, and my sin. Because God made him who knew no sin to be sin for us. That's why, for those hours on the cross, Jesus experienced the horror of being forsaken, abandoned, and rejected by God, for God's only ultimate and holy response to sin is to expel it from his presence. And Jesus went to that place of abandonment so that you and I need not do so, when we trust in Christ. He bore our sin in his own body on the tree, as Peter puts it.

That is why you and I can sing the last words of Psalm 118, words that Jesus also would have sung knowing what lay ahead the next day, but "for the joy set before him he endured the cross, scorning its shame, and sat down at the right hand of the throne of God" (Heb 12:2); we sing: "Give thanks to the Lord, for he is good; his love endures forever" (Ps 118:29).

CHAPTER TWO

PETER'S DENIAL

Matthew 26:69-75

One of my favorite books is *The Book of Heroic Failures* by Stephen Pile. Its subtitle is *The Official Handbook of the Not Terribly Good Club of Great Britain.* Here's how he introduces the book:

Success is overrated.

Everyone craves it despite daily proof that man's real genius lies in quite the opposite direction. Incompetence is what we're good at: it is the quality that marks us off from animals, and we should learn to revere it. . . .

I am sure that I am not the only one who cannot do things and the slightest investigation reveals that no one else can do anything either. . . .

So, in 1976 the Not Terribly Good Club of Great Britain was formed, with myself, cocooned in administrative failure, as president.

To qualify for membership you just had to be not terribly good at something (fishing, small talk, batik, anything) and then attend meetings at which people talked about and gave public demonstrations of the things they could not do.

In September 1976, twenty members hand-picked from all fields of incompetence gathered for the inaugural dinner at an exquisitely inferior London restaurant.

The book then goes on to describe the most spectacular failures that historical research could uncover: the most unsuccessful bank robbery, the worst bus service, the least successful fireworks display, the worst performance of *Macbeth*, the fastest defeat in a war, and so on. It is a brilliantly funny book.

But, of course, in real life failure is usually very far from funny, except sometimes when we look back on minor moments of our own fallibility. Failure can be tragic and even desperately sad. We can think of marriages that have failed, or of important exams that we failed. We think of brave rescue attempts that have tragically failed, or when somebody failed to keep a really important promise. We are even hardly surprised when politicians fail to keep the promises of their election manifesto. Failure can be disappointing, cruel, tragic—and sadly, sometimes simply predictable.

Here we have Peter's great failure. It is so significant that it is one of the few events that is recorded in all four Gospels. All four Gospels record that Jesus predicted it, and Peter did it. There it is, right in the middle of the story of the suffering and death of Jesus, making that tragic story even more painful with the realities of Judas' betrayal and Peter's denial. The greatest ever story of the redemption of the world is punctured by this moment of squalid human treachery.

Peter's failure is certainly tragic. And yet, of course, as I'm sure we'd all agree, it's very understandable. And we can identify with Peter. Surely only the most brazen of us would want to claim that we would have stood firm when Peter caved in.

Let's relive the story by taking some time to imagine the scene and put ourselves in it. Here is how Matthew tells it.

> Now Peter was sitting out in the courtyard, and a servant girl came to him. "You also were with Jesus of Galilee," she said.
>
> But he denied it before them all. "I don't know what you're talking about," he said.
>
> Then he went out to the gateway, where another servant girl saw him and said to the people there, "This fellow was with Jesus of Nazareth."
>
> He denied it again, with an oath: "I don't know the man!"
>
> After a little while, those standing there went up to Peter and said, "Surely you are one of them; your accent gives you away."
>
> Then he began to call down curses, and he swore to them, "I don't know the man!"
>
> Immediately a rooster crowed. Then Peter remembered the word Jesus had spoken: "Before the rooster crows, you will disown me three times." And he went outside and wept bitterly. (Mt 26:69-75)

Matthew's story is full of irony and shock. Look at the contrasting images he puts before us when we set the Peter incident in the context of the rest of Matthew 26.

There, on the one hand, is Jesus—in danger of losing his life, and yet he stands firm under threats before the highest authorities in the land. And there, on the other hand, is Peter—in danger of probably not very much except embarrassment and possibly a bit of a beating, but he gives way in front of nothing more than a couple of servant girls.

There, on the one hand, is Jesus—put on oath to speak the truth about himself, and he does so. And there, on the other hand, is Peter—calling down oaths in order to deny the truth about himself and Jesus.

There, on the one hand, is Jesus—falsely accused of blasphemy (an incredible thing in itself: the Son of God accused of blasphemy!). And there, on the other hand, is Peter—actually guilty of blasphemy in the very presence of the Lord. In fact, the text not only says that he falsely swore an oath (taking the name of the Lord in vain in order to tell a lie), but it also says "he began to call down curses" (Mt 26:74). Some Bible translations add "on himself," but the New International Version just says that he called down curses. It's perfectly possibly that he called down curses on Jesus, saying something like, "I swear to God I don't know him. Curse the fellow!" How awful!

On the one hand, Peter curses and swear his way out of it when a *slave girl* looks at him with threatening recognition. On the other hand, when *Jesus* looks at him (as Luke tells us), Peter can only rush out into the darkness as the rooster is crowing, reminding him of the words of Jesus.

So here is Peter, the antihero of our story. Peter, the man who wielded a sword in the darkness of the garden in front of a squad of soldiers just a few hours beforehand. And yet he withers before a servant girl in the light of a fire. Peter, the man who could haul in a whole net full of fish singlehandedly. And yet he melts in fear before a few suspicious questions. Peter, the man who swore that he would die for Jesus. And yet here he is, swearing that he doesn't even know him. Peter, the man who was so full of courage and good intentions just a couple of hours before this. And yet now he's full of shame, bitterness, deep despair, and overflowing tears. Peter, the rock, Jesus had called him. And now he's just a sobbing blob of jelly. In short, Peter failed. Suddenly, surprisingly, shatteringly—Peter failed.

And as far as Matthew's Gospel goes, that's it. Of course, we know more about Peter after this from the other Gospels, but as far as Matthew's Gospel goes, Peter never reappears. Peter is last seen out in the darkness weeping and gnashing his teeth. End of story (in Matthew).

So, what does it tell us? How do we respond, not only to what this story tells us about Peter, but also to what it tells us for ourselves? Why has Matthew reported it? Why have all the Gospels reported this story? I think it tells us three things, at the least: failure is a fact, failure is foreseen, and failure is forgiven.

FAILURE IS A FACT

Failure is a fact in the Bible. Think about it. Do a mental scan through the Bible. Adam and Eve failed, even though they were in a perfect environment. Abraham failed; he told lies about his wife and abused Hagar. Samuel failed to get his own sons to behave properly, even though he started out his own career condemning Eli for the same thing. Gideon failed, even after his great victory over the Midianites, when he said he wouldn't become a king and then behaved as if he was one and made an idolatrous object. Moses failed in the wilderness, to his own great regret. David failed appallingly, not only in his acts of adultery and planned murder, but in failing to control his own family during the rest of his life. Every king of Israel failed in one way or another. The people of Israel as a whole—God's covenant people, God's redeemed people—failed for generation after generation through the Old Testament. Failure runs through the Old Testament like a ragged thread.

The New Testament shows us people failing all over the place as well. Even in this story, why is it that we blame Peter for *his* denial of Jesus when, in fact, Matthew tells us that *all of the disciples* forsook him and fled? Peter, poor man, was the only one (well, almost the only one, as we'll see) who was actually in a position where he *could* deny Jesus. The only reason the other disciples didn't deny Jesus is that they weren't even there! They had fled. And yet, as Matthew tells us very carefully in Matthew 26:35, they had *all* said the same thing as Peter to Jesus: "We won't disown you, we won't deny you." But when it came to the crunch, they all deserted him except for Peter and (as we'll see) one other. It was a collective failure.

The whole Bible, from beginning to end, is a story of human failure (with the single exception of the Lord Jesus Christ himself). In fact, you could say that the title of Stephen Pile's book would be a very good title for the Bible—*The Book of Heroic Failures*—except that most failures in the Bible weren't particularly heroic. Certainly, its subtitle would fit the Bible—"The Official Handbook of the Not Terribly Good Club of Humanity"—except that the Bible doesn't tell us just that we're not terribly good. It actually tells us that we're radically and terribly flawed. Sin has wormed its evil way into the depths of our human nature. Indeed, mere failure is only one of the least of our problems. Genesis 6 tells us that God saw that "every inclination of the thoughts of the human heart was only evil all the time" (Gen 6:5). Jeremiah observed, probably from his own honest knowledge of himself: "The heart is deceitful above all things and beyond cure. Who can understand it?" (Jer 17:9). Paul tells us that, whether you're a good Jew or a wicked pagan, it doesn't make any difference: "There is no difference between Jew and Gentile, for all have sinned and fall short of the glory of God" (Rom 3:22-23). John tells us: "If we claim to be without sin, we deceive ourselves and the truth is not in us" (1 Jn 1:8).

So if you're ever tempted to imagine that you've never really failed, get real! You're only deceiving yourself. Failure is a fact. It's certainly a fact in the Bible.

Failure is a fact of experience. Most of us have some idea of the great story of the history of the Christian church. We know that the gospel has spread from country to country and from continent to continent. We know something of the origins and growth of the great missionary movements. Maybe we've read some missionary biographies and admire the great things that courageous people have done for God down through the centuries. We can tell that great story of the past two thousand years as a testimony to the success of the gospel by the power, grace, and sovereignty of God.

But viewed from another angle, church history is also a history of failures—some of them pretty terrible. Rather like the stories of the Old Testament, they sometimes make us stand in amazement at what God accomplished *in spite of* the weaknesses and failures of the people he used, rather than *because of* their marvelous achievements. Sometimes (unlike the Bible) missionary biographies gloss over those less inspiring moments of failure.

I have another book of heroic failures. This one's actually rather bigger than Stephen Pile's little paperback. It's called *Too Valuable to Lose: Exploring the Causes and Cures of Missionary Attrition.* "Attrition" is the rather polite word that's used for missionaries who return home earlier than they expected or originally intended, for whatever reason. The book has researched those reasons and sought to analyze and address them. It is the product of an extensive research project, followed by a conference that was held at All Nations Christian College some years ago, to examine the reality of missionary failure (or apparent failure).

But missionaries? Here are people who, we might think, have the very highest motivation and calling, and all good intentions, to serve God in Christian mission. Some of them have had intensive training. Most of them are strongly supported and prayed for by others. And yet some of them also fail in one way or another. Some of them return home broken and disillusioned. Some fall into ungodly relationships. Some fall ill. Some just give up. The reasons are very varied, and not all of them are in any way blameworthy.

Failure is a fact. Let's face it. The great tragedy is that so often we don't, or we won't, admit it. And, to be honest, we're usually rather embarrassed when other Christians start confessing their failures, in case we have to join the confession with a few of our own. We'd rather cover up our shame and keep up some sort of pretense of "victorious Christian living," "Spirit-filled Christian living," or whatever phrase is popular at the time.

After all, we've read the books. We've been to the conferences. We've been up at the front or down on our backs. We've been there, done that, got the T-shirt, all in the effort to be a successful Christian.

So we're not about to admit, after all that, that we still haven't got it all together. We're not going to admit that we still fall for the same old sins. We're not going to admit that we don't like being too visible as a Christian. We wouldn't go so far as to say we've ever actually *denied* knowing Christ; we just don't say much about it at all. We're not going to admit the way we talk and think when nobody is listening, or what we look at when we're on our own, or the way we treat those closest to us in our own families.

We're not going to admit that, in short, we still fail. But fail we do. And we know it.

It grieves me that in some Christian churches and communities there seems to be a whole culture of pretense, a constant celebration of glittering success stories ("testimonies"), and a denial of the reality of failure. I think it can be pastorally disastrous, and it can even come close to denying the truth of the gospel. I have been in worship services where there was no confession of sin at all in the whole service, nothing but a diet of triumphant songs and testimonies and the preaching of "success," "faith," and "victory."

Have you ever reflected on this odd paradox in some Christian circles? It seems that *in order to become* a Christian, the *first* thing you have to do is to admit that you've failed. But somehow, *once you have become* a Christian, the *last* thing you're ever expected to do is to admit that you fail. It seems that in order to enter the church, you must accept that you're a sinner, but the only way of staying credible within the church is by pretending to be a success. Isn't there something wrong there? Aren't we missing something of the ongoing reality of grace in our lives—not just at the moment of coming to faith, but in every step of the journey that follows?

Let's come back to our story of Peter. Surely, I think, one of the reasons why this story is in the Bible (recorded four times) is that it forces us to admit and accept the reality of failure. This is a very liberating thing to do. Peter—one of the foremost of the first disciples of Jesus—failed. I fail. You fail. And so does every other Christian on the planet. What a relief! Because, you see, the truly liberating thing that this story tells us is not only that failure is a fact, but also that failure is foreseen.

FAILURE IS FORESEEN

One of the shocking points of Matthew's account in chapter 26 is that both the betrayal by Judas and the denial by Peter were predicted by Jesus.

Look at Matthew 26:21: Jesus says, "Truly I tell you, one of you will betray me." And they were all appalled and shocked, and said, "It couldn't be me! What, me? No way! Not me, for sure!" It was a huge surprise, and apparently even at this stage none of the rest of the disciples suspected Judas.

Then look at Matthew 26:31: Jesus says, "This very night you will all fall away on account of me." Another big shock! And they all said, "No, no, no! Of course we won't!" Especially Peter, who says, "Me? Never! I won't disown you, even if all these others do! You know me, Lord! I'll die for you if I have to!" To which Jesus replies, "This very night, before the rooster crows, you will disown me three times" (Mt 26:34).

The failure of Judas and Peter (and of all the others too, of course) was foreseen by Jesus. Tragically, that fact seems to have made no difference for Judas, but as far as Peter is concerned, I think it is probably what saved him. Even as he went outside into the dark and wept bitterly, he must have been remembering, "Jesus knew! Jesus said I would do that." That probably made his tears all the more bitter. And think of that look the Lord gave him (Lk 22:61). Peter knew that Jesus knew what he had just done—but Jesus had known all along. Indeed, Jesus had quoted Scripture (Mt 26:31) to show that even Peter's denial and the desertion of all the disciples were in some mysterious way a fulfilment of what the Scripture had said. So the whole scene was, therefore, in some sense, still under control. Jesus had it covered in more ways than one.

An old hymn has the line, "Jesus knows our every weakness." That's not a putdown. It's not a veiled threat. It's a word of comfort. Because if Jesus *knows*, then Jesus can cope with it. There is hope. There is light at the end of the tunnel. Failure is foreseen. So our failures certainly *grieve* the Lord, but they don't *surprise* him because he knows what's in us. He knows what we are capable of.

I wonder if you've ever reflected on the way the story of the prediction of Peter's denial is told in John's Gospel. I find it really quite remarkable. John 13 is a narrative filled with emotional tension. There's painful embarrassment as Jesus washes the disciples' feet. Then there's the shock of the prediction of the betrayal and the mysterious word about how Jesus is going to leave them. And finally there's the shock of Jesus predicting that Peter will deny him. Peter protests, but Jesus insists, "Will you really lay down your life for me? Very truly I tell you, before the rooster crows, you will disown me three times!" (Jn 13:38).

Remember, in John's original writing there were no chapter divisions. There was no heading, as in our Bibles, announcing, "Chapter 14 verse 1, Jesus Comforts His Disciples." Those breaks and titles were added much later to help us find our way around the Bible. Unfortunately, they sometimes make us read from the start of what we now call John 14 as if it has nothing to do with what we've just read in chapter 13. But in John's Gospel as John originally wrote it, Jesus went straight on from all that had just been said at the end of chapter 13 to say, "do not let your hearts be troubled" (Jn 14:1).

What?! How could he say that, after what had just happened? Jesus is saying, "One of you is going to betray me, I'm going to die for you, one of you is going to deny me . . . but listen: don't let your hearts be troubled! Don't worry. Don't panic. Trust me. You trust in God, so trust me. I know what I'm doing. I know where I'm going. And even your betrayals and your denials cannot destroy or derail what I am now about to do for you and for the world. I know all about what's going to happen, so don't let your hearts be troubled."

Failure is foreseen, and Jesus can be trusted even in the midst of it. That is what leads to the third and last thing that Peter discovered in this story (actually, this happens after this story as Matthew tells it; in Matthew's Gospel, this is the last we see of Peter, but the other Gospels give us a happier ending). Peter discovered that not only is failure a fact, not only is failure foreseen, but also failure is forgiven.

FAILURE IS FORGIVEN

Peter's tears were undoubtedly tears of remorse. But they must also have been tears of repentance that led ultimately to Peter's restoration. How did that happen? Luke and John give us the answers. Luke tells us how Jesus prayed for Peter's faith, and John tells us how Jesus probed for Peter's love. Those two things were the keys to Peter's restoration.

Jesus prayed for Peter's faith (Lk 22:31-32). Luke records that, just before warning Peter that he would deny him three times, Jesus said to Peter, "Simon, Simon, Satan has asked to sift all of you as wheat. But I have prayed for you, Simon, that your faith may not fail. And when you have turned back, strengthen your brothers." And that prayer of Jesus was surely answered.

Yes, of course, Peter's nerve failed. Yes, Peter's courage failed. But somehow, Peter's faith did not fail. I don't know how, and I don't suppose that Peter knew how either, but somehow and somewhere inside himself, Peter went on trusting Jesus, even through this ghastly, shattering experience. Peter's faith didn't fail, because Jesus prayed that it wouldn't. I wonder, even as he went out into the darkness, whether Peter heard in his ears not just the taunts of the people he was running away from, but also the echo of those words of Jesus just a few hours before: "You trust in God. Trust also in me. . . . Trust me, Peter. Go on having faith in me as you did on that first day you followed me. Trust me. Trust me."

Have you failed Jesus? Of course you have. The more appropriate question to ask would be: When did you most recently fail Jesus? Then the key question is: Do you still trust Jesus?

Have you let Jesus down again? Of course you have. Of course I have. The question is: Do you still trust him?

Have you felt the deep shame of that failure? And the embarrassment of it? Have you found yourself almost unable to face Jesus in prayer again because of it? Of course you have. The question is: Do you still trust Jesus?

After all, it was when you first decided to trust Jesus, when you first chose to put your faith in him, that you began your life as a Christian. Why stop trusting him now in the face of this latest failure, when you've trusted him to carry on the cross all the failures and sins of all your life?

The older I get and the longer I go on in the Christian life, and the more times I experience my own personal failure—usually known only to myself but sometimes to others—the more I learn how important it is not to trust myself, but to constantly come back and say, "Lord, it's *you* I trust." You see, Peter thought he could trust himself, didn't he? He protested boldly that *he* would never let Jesus down. He would go to prison! He would die! But deny Jesus? Never! Peter trusted his own courage, his own strength. But he fell flat on his face, devastated and disgraced. The question is: Where do you go from there? The answer is: you go back to Jesus, who's praying for you, praying that your faith will survive. Peter knew that he could still trust Jesus even if he could not have seen or imagined what that might mean. Peter's restoration depended on his continuing faith, and that depended on God's assured answer to Jesus' prayer.

Jesus probed for Peter's love (Jn 21:15-19). Jesus not only prayed for Peter's faith, but also, he probed for Peter's love. That comes out in this story at the end of John's Gospel. It's a very familiar story; we know it well. Jesus makes breakfast for the disciples after they're done fishing, and after yet another miracle involving a lot of fish. And then, when they've all eaten, and perhaps as they are starting to walk away from the lake, Jesus asks this question three times to Peter, once and again and again: "Peter, do you love me?"

I rather think that this was in private conversation as they walked, for we read that "Peter turned and saw that the disciple whom Jesus loved was following them" (Jn 21:20), which suggests that Jesus and Peter were walking together, with John just behind them, possibly the only one able to hear the conversation between Jesus and Peter. Of course, I can't be sure of that, and it is also possible that the conversation happened with all the disciples listening, and before Jesus said (yet again), "Follow me!" (Jn 21:19).

But no matter exactly how the scene unfolded, have you ever wondered why it's only John who brings us the story of Peter's restoration? Why John? The answer, I feel sure, is that it was because John was the only one who witnessed Peter's failure (apart from Jesus, of course).

In John 18, Jesus has just been arrested by the soldiers in the garden and is being taken off, bound, to the Jewish high court.

> Simon Peter and another disciple were following Jesus. Because this disciple was known to the high priest, he went with Jesus into the high priest's courtyard, but Peter had to wait outside at the door. The other disciple, who was known to the high priest, came back, spoke to the servant girl on duty there and brought Peter in. (Jn 18:15-16)

That phrase "the other disciple" is usually assumed to mean John himself. It is John's anonymous signature for himself. He uses it a number of times in the Gospel: "The other disciple whom Jesus loved." So almost certainly, it was John who was known to the high priest, who came back, spoke to the girl on duty at the door, and let Peter into the courtyard where Jesus was on trial before Annas and then Caiaphas the high priest.

So John was there. And John saw, and John heard, this horrifying moment of Peter's cursing denial of Jesus. John actually watched as Peter disowned Jesus, again and again. John heard Peter saying that he didn't even know Jesus; this Jesus whom they both loved; this Jesus for whom they had both given up everything three years earlier. Peter, James, and John were the innermost group of disciples, remember? Hadn't they walked and talked and eaten with Jesus? Hadn't Jesus even visited Peter's own house and healed his wife's mother? Hadn't Peter been the one to solemnly affirm that this Jesus was the Messiah, the Son of God? Hadn't they climbed the Mount of Transfiguration together with Jesus? And hadn't Jesus got down and washed Peter's feet just a few hours before? And now, here is John watching Peter with jaw-dropping astonishment, as the fellow denies—again and again—that he even knows Jesus at all, and does it with oaths and blasphemy and cursing, with his coarse Galilean accent giving him away all the time.

John was there! I sometimes wonder how Peter and John ever faced each other again after that terrible night. There must have been agonizing moments between them on the Saturday after the crucifixion. Did Peter beg John not to tell the other disciples? How could Peter ever again talk about loving Jesus if John were around and listening? And yet, that is exactly what happened. And John is the one who tells us about it.

It didn't happen because of Peter's initiative, but under Jesus' probing, surgical question—"Peter, do you love me? Do you love me more than these? Peter, do you love me?"—asked three times, like the three times Peter denied Jesus. The connection is obvious. Jesus knows, Peter knows. And John is listening.

But who is this asking the question? This is from John chapter 21, which means this is the *risen* Jesus now. This is the Jesus who has already been on the cross and in the tomb. This is the Jesus who had taken upon himself all of Peter's guilt, failure, disgrace, humiliation, and sin. All of Peter's shame had been carried by Jesus on the cross. And all of your shame. And all of mine as well.

Bearing shame and scoffing rude,
In my place condemned he stood;
Sealed my pardon with his blood.
Hallelujah! What a Savior!

And this is the Jesus who asks the question, "Now then, Peter, do you love me?" And Peter says, "Lord, Lord, you know. You *know*. You know I love you. I've *always* loved you, and I still do. Even when I was denying you, I loved you. It broke my heart and yours. I hated myself, but I loved you. And I love you now, Lord. I love you, Lord."

And that's all Jesus wanted to hear this time around. Not all that swearing that he would die for him (which he would do eventually). Not all that great bluster, "Me? No, no, I'll never deny you!" All Jesus wanted to hear was, "Lord, you know that I love you."

And that was all John needed to hear as well. For if Jesus had forgiven Peter, then John must too. He could love Peter again as they both loved Jesus. And that's why John recorded it for the rest of us. *So Peter the failure becomes Peter the forgiven.*

Have you been there? I have. I know what it is in my own experience, after an episode of particular and despicable failure of the Lord, to be literally flat on my face on the floor in tears before the Lord Jesus Christ, saying to him again and again, "Lord, I love you. Lord, have mercy on me. Lord, forgive me. I want to go on serving you, if you will allow it. Lord, forgive me. Lord restore me," and clinging to Psalms 32 and 51. And then, too, I know what it is to get up from that experience, deeply repentant, deeply chastened, but knowing that the prayer is answered, knowing the warm relief of forgiveness and cleansing for the sins that have been washed away by the blood of Christ.

That's the story of Peter's denial. It's a shocking story. But in the end, you see, it's a *safe* story. It is safe because of where it is, embedded here in the story of the cross. Yes, Peter's failure, like yours and mine, was a *fact* that he would never deny. Peter's failure, like yours and mine, was *foreseen* by Jesus. But, most important of all, Peter's failure was *forgiven*, like yours and mine can be, because of the atoning, healing, and cleansing blood of the cross.

That is why this story is in the gospel. Because it is good news.

REFLECTION

I'm sure that the Holy Spirit of God through his Word in this chapter has touched your heart. And the question is, what will you do with that moving of the Spirit in your heart and conscience? Knowing, as we all do, that one way or another we have failed Jesus, in small things or in great things; we have disowned him and failed him again and again—perhaps even, for some of us, in ways that are profound and significant, in things of which we are deeply, deeply ashamed. Perhaps there are tears to be shed about that. But that's all right. You are not in the courtyard of the high priest. You are not being mocked. You are not on trial. You are in the presence of God and the Holy Spirit. So bring whatever is on your heart and open it up to the Lord. He knows it anyway. He's known it all along. So don't hide it any more. And hear the question of Jesus: "Do you love me? Do you trust me?" Come back again to the cross and to the blood of the Lord Jesus Christ for his forgiveness. Because the John who told us that if we say that we have not sinned, we are deceiving ourselves and the truth is not in us—that same John says that if we confess our sins, God is faithful and just, will forgive our sins, and cleanse us from all unrighteousness. That is the gospel promise. Come back to that and receive it and hear again that word of forgiveness from the Lord Jesus Christ himself.

CHAPTER THREE

INSULTS AND PARADISE

Luke 23:26–43

As the soldiers led him away, they seized Simon from Cyrene, who was on his way in from the country, and put the cross on him and made him carry it behind Jesus. A large number of people followed him, including women who mourned and wailed for him. Jesus turned and said to them, "Daughters of Jerusalem, do not weep for me; weep for yourselves and for your children. For the time will come when you will say, 'Blessed are the childless women, the wombs that never bore and the breasts that never nursed!' Then

"'they will say to the mountains, "Fall on us!"
and to the hills, "Cover us!"'

For if people do these things when the tree is green, what will happen when it is dry?"

Two other men, both criminals, were also led out with him to be executed. When they came to the place called the Skull, they crucified him there, along with the criminals—one on his right, the other on his left. Jesus said, "Father, forgive them, for they do not know what they are doing." And they divided up his clothes by casting lots.

The people stood watching, and the rulers even sneered at him. They said, "He saved others; let him save himself if he is God's Messiah, the Chosen One."

The soldiers also came up and mocked him. They offered him wine vinegar and said, "If you are the king of the Jews, save yourself."

There was a written notice above him, which read: THIS IS THE KING OF THE JEWS.

One of the criminals who hung there hurled insults at him: "Aren't you the Messiah? Save yourself and us!"

But the other criminal rebuked him. "Don't you fear God," he said, "since you are under the same sentence? We are punished justly, for we are getting what our deeds deserve. But this man has done nothing wrong."

Then he said, "Jesus, remember me when you come into your kingdom."

Jesus answered him, "Truly I tell you, today you will be with me in paradise." (Lk 23:26-43)

"We preach Christ crucified," said the apostle Paul (1 Cor 1:23). That sounds very simple—just one thing to talk about (though clearly Paul did not mean it in a strictly literal sense—he did talk and write about many things, but they all centered on the gospel of the crucified and risen Christ). And yet, as we look at the story of the cross in Luke's Gospel, it is a remarkable combination of the simple and the profound. I marvel at Luke's skill in the way he presents this gripping story in such a simple, unadorned, and unsensational way, and yet, at the same time, he weaves into it some profound textures of understanding and scriptural meaning for his readers.

Even with just a surface reading of this passage, you can get the point of what Luke is telling us. From these few short verses of chapter 23 we can summarize what Luke tells us as follows: this man Jesus of Nazareth was innocent of all wrongdoing; he was executed unjustly, but he died forgiving his enemies; he died promising eternal life to a repentant sinner; he died to save even those who taunted him that he couldn't save himself. There is gospel truth in that short surface summary of Luke's narrative.

But beneath that simple story, Luke invites us to see some greater depths of meaning and truth that challenge us and encourage us. First of all, let's examine four scenes that are filled with Scripture; second, three temptations that are filled with irony; and finally, two sayings that are filled with hope.

FOUR SCENES FULL OF SCRIPTURE

Let's examine these four scenes that Luke puts before us, scenes that are so filled with the Scriptures. At one level, Luke simply reports the events. He just recounts four things that happened during those dreadful hours before and during the crucifixion of Jesus. And yet, as he does so, Luke either directly quotes from some Old Testament Scriptures or hints at very well-known texts from the Old Testament, in a way that colors in the significance of what he describes.

Scene 1: The weeping women (Lk 23:26-31; Scripture echo: Hos 10:8). Jesus is on his way to the place of crucifixion. Simon is carrying the heavy crossbar that Jesus will be nailed to, and the women who are accompanying him are weeping, wailing, and crying out until Jesus stops and speaks to them. He says to them, "Don't weep for *me*—weep for *yourselves*, because much worse than this is going to happen in this city."

This is now the fourth time in the Gospel of Luke that Jesus has explicitly predicted the coming siege and destruction of Jerusalem that did indeed take place in AD 70, about forty years after his death. You can read the other predictions in Luke 13:34-35, 19:41-44, and 21:20-24. What Jesus means in Luke 23:29 is that, when that event happens, those women who are now pitied because they have no children will actually be considered lucky because they'll have no extra mouths to feed in the siege, and they won't have to go through the pain of watching their children suffer and die of hunger or be slain by enemy soldiers.

Then Jesus quotes from Hosea 10:8, a text that spoke of the time when Samaria, the capital city of the northern kingdom of Israel, had been destroyed by the Assyrians. That happened in 721 BC and had been foretold by Hosea and Amos. So Jesus takes that text from the past and applies it to the future. "It will happen again for Jerusalem just like that: people will wish the mountains would fall on them, because they'd rather be dead and buried than suffer in the siege and all the destruction that will follow."

Then Jesus quotes a proverbial saying in Luke 23:31 about green wood and dry wood. Most likely, the proverb meant something like this: "If you think this is bad, far worse is to come." And Jesus means: "It may be horrible to watch what is happening to me now, but worse is to come for those who ultimately reject God and reject God's Savior." And indeed, that verse Jesus quoted from Hosea 10:8 is also found in Revelation 6:16. There it becomes the cry of those who will face the wrath and judgment of God on the terrible final day of judgment. They will want to be buried rather than face the wrath of God, but they will not be able to escape.

So you see, Jesus is saying—even at the moment of his own impending death—that there is worse to come. And that worse moment is not just the near future (the destruction of Jerusalem in AD 70), but the ultimate future, the final judgment itself. In response, either we will find shelter under the cross on which Jesus bore God's judgment for us, or we will find no shelter from the judgment of God when we stand before him on the last day.

Scene 2: The heartless soldiers (Lk 23:32-34; Scripture echo: Ps 22:18). Luke does not dwell on the appalling, calculated cruelty of crucifixion. He just reports it ("they crucified him there") without any mention of the blood, sweat, excrement, and flies, the excruciating agony, the shameful nakedness, and the prolonged dehydrating torture that it was. He was writing during the Roman Empire. People knew what crucifixion was. They didn't need details.

But what about those who carried it out—the Roman soldiers? Really, it was all just in a day's work for them. They'd have done it many times before. It was just three more wretches to bang nails into and hoist up on their crosses to die. The soldiers were casual, they were callous, and they had no idea who it was they were brutalizing; that was more than soldiers needed to know. Probably a few terrorists, they thought, and good riddance. And when they'd done their work, they just sat down to wait. It could take a crucified man several days to die, unless you hurried them along by breaking their legs so they couldn't heave themselves up and keep breathing. So a spot of gambling would relieve the boredom. They gathered up the only earthly possessions Jesus had—his clothing that had been stripped off his back already. That would fetch a few shekels in the market later for the lucky soldier who won the gamble.

So Luke simply tells us "they divided up his clothes by casting lots." But anyone with "ears to hear" would know that this was an echo of Psalm 22.

This is the psalm that opens with the words, "My God, my God, why have you forsaken me?" Mark tells us that Jesus cried out those words during his crucifixion (Mk 15:34), and Luke knew Mark's Gospel. But this is also the psalm that finishes with the words, "They will proclaim his righteousness, declaring to a people yet unborn: He has done it!" (Ps 22:31). And John tells us that Jesus cried out similar words at the climax of his suffering, before he laid down his life and breathed his last: "It is finished" (Jn 19:30; we shall consider what that means in chapter 5).

So this psalm, from beginning to end, was already filling the consciousness of Jesus. It was in his heart and mind and on his lips. Here is just a short extract:

> Dogs surround me,
>> a pack of villains encircles me;
>> they pierce my hands and my feet.
> All my bones are on display;
>> people stare and gloat over me.
> They divide my clothes among them
>> and cast lots for my garment. (Ps 22:16-18)

That is the echo Luke intends us to hear. This psalm expresses the kind of suffering Jesus was enduring at that moment. But it also expresses confidence in God because, although Jesus died in agony, he did not die in despair. The very next verses say, "But you, Lord, do not be far from me. . . . Deliver me from the sword [or "death"]" (Ps 22:19-20). And indeed God would do exactly that; not in the sense that Jesus was delivered *from* dying, but that God delivered him *through* death—Jesus' very real death—by the power of his resurrection. The psalm goes on to celebrate how God's victory would be celebrated throughout the earth and draw people from all nations to come and worship him (Ps 22:27). Psalm 22 speaks of both appalling suffering and incredible triumph!

So, through the soldiers' greedy gambling, Luke points us to a Scripture that is highly significant in interpreting the meaning of Christ's death and the future that it would lead to.

Scene 3: The mocking bystanders (Lk 23:35-39; Scripture echo: Ps 69:21). Almost everybody seems to have been mocking and taunting Jesus. As the soldiers joined in this mockery, they added a gesture. They offered some wine vinegar to Jesus. John tells us that someone dipped a sponge in it and lifted it up on a stick to Jesus' mouth when he gasped that he was thirsty (Jn 19:28-29). But Luke just mentions the vinegar and puts it in the context of mockery.

Once again, it seems, Luke is hinting at yet another psalm, Psalm 69, treating it like a lens through which to understand what was happening. It is another psalm by someone who was going through unjust suffering and cruelty. And in the midst of that suffering, the psalmist cries out to God,

> You know how I am scorned, disgraced and shamed;
>> all my enemies are before you.
> Scorn has broken my heart
>> and has left me helpless;
> I looked for sympathy, but there was none,
>> for comforters, but I found none.
> They put gall in my food
>> and gave me vinegar for my thirst. (Ps 69:19-21)

But read the rest of that psalm. You'll find that the one who has suffered so much confidently expects God to bring him salvation in the end, and by the end of Psalm 69 even calls on heaven and earth to praise God. Yet again, as with the echo of Psalm 22, Luke wants us to understand that, when we see the things that happened around the death of Christ, they remind us of Scriptures that show us that all is not lost. There is hope, God is still in charge, and we will still have reason to praise him.

Scene 4: The repentant criminal (Lk 23:40-43; Scripture echo: Is 53:6-9). All four Gospels tell us that there were two other men crucified alongside Jesus, one on each side of him. Luke says they were criminals. Matthew and Mark use a word that described the political zealots, the freedom fighters of that day—the guerrillas who killed Romans whenever they could. In our day they would probably be called terrorists. The Romans would have thought of them as violent religious extremists.

But one of them recognizes the injustice of what is happening, and he speaks words that at one level express a simple fact, but at another level express a theology that is far more profound than he could have understood. The condemned terrorist says, "We are punished justly, for we are getting what our deeds deserve. But this man has done nothing wrong" (Lk 23:41). What he means is, "*We* are guilty, but *he* is innocent. Whatever he is dying for, it is not for his own sins."

I think Luke almost certainly wants us to hear in those words of the criminal an echo of Isaiah 53. We know these familiar words about the servant of the Lord:

> But he was pierced for our transgressions,
>> he was crushed for our iniquities;
> the punishment that brought us peace was on him,
>> and by his wounds we are healed.
> We all, like sheep, have gone astray,
>> each of us has turned to our own way;
> and the Lord has laid on him
>> the iniquity of us all. . . .
>
> though he had done no violence,
>> nor was any deceit in his mouth. (Is 53:5-6, 9)

Jesus on the cross was not suffering the punishment *he* deserved (like the two criminals on either side of him), but suffering for our sake, bearing our sins. Of course, the criminal who said what he did could not have understood all this (though maybe he understood more than we think, in view of his next request), but Luke did, and he lets us hear the echoes of Scripture as he records the words spoken.

So Luke has given us four scenes of things that happened or were said as Jesus went to the cross. At one level they are what we might call circumstantial detail, just part of the story because they happened. But by quoting or echoing the Scriptures, Luke is leading us to realize what Paul wrote (and doubtless Luke had heard this from Paul since they were close companions): "that Christ died for our sins *according to the Scriptures*" (1 Cor 15:3, emphasis mine). That means, the death of Christ was in accordance with, in fulfilment of, and in line with the Scriptures of the Old Testament. But of course, Paul went straight on to say "that he was buried, that he was raised on the third day *according to the Scriptures*" (1 Cor 15:4, emphasis mine). And in his very next chapter (Luke 24), Luke will show us explicitly, through the mouth of the risen Jesus himself, how not only the death but also the resurrection of Jesus happened "as it is written" in accordance with the Scriptures. So Luke's four scenes are full of echoes of Scripture that deepen our understanding of what was happening at the cross of Christ.

Let's examine what exactly was said in those three taunts that different people hurled at Jesus.

THREE LAST TEMPTATIONS FULL OF IRONY

Within his narrative Luke embeds what I think can rightly be called the three last temptations of Christ. I don't think that's too strong a phrase because three times we read of people taunting

Jesus with the words, "Let him save himself . . . save yourself. . . . Save yourself and us!" (Lk 23:35, 37, 39). I think Luke records these three times as a deliberate reminder of the narrative of Jesus' temptations by the devil in the wilderness (Lk 4:1-13).

Those three temptations of the devil had a similar force. The devil said to Jesus, "*If* you are the Son of God. . . . *If* you are the Son of God" (Lk 4:3, 9, emphasis mine). And now at the cross, the same taunting, doubting, mocking question is framed: "If he is God's Messiah, the Chosen One. . . . If you are the king of the Jews. . . . Aren't you the Messiah?" (Lk 23:35, 37, 39). And of course, all Jesus had to do to prove that that was exactly who he was would have been to burst forth from the cross with a great miraculous demonstration of his power, just as Satan had tempted him to do in the wilderness.

Back in the wilderness, the temptations of Satan had been aimed at getting Jesus to avoid the way of obedience as the Son of God, the way that would lead him to suffering and death. The devil dangled before Jesus the enticement of political power, some spectacular religious demonstration, or some miraculous appeal to the hungry masses. Anything but going to death. And those temptations lasted all through his ministry. It was not just the devil who tried to divert Jesus from what he had come to do. Peter tried at Caesarea Philippi. Jesus' own family urged him to come home and stop getting into trouble. Even Pontius Pilate wanted to release him. And in his own human vulnerability in the garden of Gethsemane, he begged God to be spared the fate that lay ahead of him but resisted that option with the words "yet not my will, but yours be done" (Lk 22:42). And even now—at the very last, when he is actually nailed to the cross—those temptations return with fierce force. The devil tries yet again in triple repetition. If only he can get Jesus to save himself and come down from the cross, then Jesus' whole mission of saving the world will be lost.

And so the tempter speaks through three different groups of people who had nothing whatsoever in common with one another. Indeed, some of them were enemies of each other, except that now they all had one common enemy: Jesus. They all say the same thing, but they all mean it in quite different ways. And in each case, there is a rich irony between what they *think* they are saying and the actual *truth* of the situation.

The religious rulers (Lk 23:35). First, the religious rulers sneer at Jesus, "He saved others; let him save himself *if* he is God's Messiah, the Chosen One" (emphasis mine). Their mockery is a rejection of the *claims* of Jesus. "He thinks he's the Messiah, does he? He thinks he's God's Chosen One, does he? He thinks he's the Savior, does he?" And they laugh at the whole idea, since look where he is now: spiked on a Roman cross, powerless to save himself, let alone anybody else.

But, of course, that is exactly what Jesus was and is: God's chosen Messiah and Savior. The tragic irony is that these religious rulers both *state* the truth about Jesus and *reject* the truth about Jesus in the same breath. How dangerous and scary is that?

The Roman soldiers (Lk 23:36-38). Second, the Roman soldiers join in the taunts. Their mockery is a rejection of the *charge* that has been made against Jesus: that he is supposed to be the king of the Jews. Those were the words that were nailed up on the cross just above his head. "But that's ridiculous!" the soldiers say, laughing. "King of the Jews? Look at you now! Some king you are, stuck up there with thorns for a crown and a cross for a throne!"

Yet again, the irony of the situation is that what they said, and what had been written on the charge sheet, was simply stating the truth. Jesus was and is the King. The messianic King. Not just the King of the Jews, but the King of the Universe. That scribbled notice above Jesus on the cross was the very first piece of writing ever made about him. In fact, it was the *only* piece of writing made about him in his earthly lifetime (since all the New Testament documents were written after his resurrection): that piece of wood or parchment that was tacked up above his head stating, "This is the king of the Jews." Ironically, it stated the charge that the soldiers laughingly rejected, but it was actually truer than they could ever have known.

The terrorist (Lk 23:39). Then, third, there's one of the two criminals, who also taunts Jesus and hurls insults at him. His mockery is an attack on the *failure* of Jesus, as he sees it. He is chiding and accusing Jesus, as if to say, "Look, you should have joined *us* if you'd been any kind of real Messiah. See, you had your chance a week ago when all the crowds cheered you into Jerusalem, but you blew that chance and sneaked off somewhere. But now you've got one last chance to prove you really are the Messiah—right now! Save yourself! Save yourself—and save us too while you're about it, and then we'll leap down off these crosses and fight the Romans. Ha ha! As if . . . !" He mocks Jesus for failing to be what he thinks a Messiah should be and do.

Of course, the irony is that the only way Jesus could be the Messiah that God had planned was by *not* saving himself, and by going through that suffering and death. Only by Jesus staying on the cross to the end could God save even terrorists like them, as one of them found a few moments later.

Three taunts, three temptations, three ironies. And within all this there are also two profound paradoxes—surprises, things that are not at all what we expect.

First of all, think about the paradox of power. The three voices that taunted Jesus represent three different kinds of human power that confronted Jesus at the cross.

First, there is the power of *religious establishment:* those religious rulers. They know and boast of their own power at this moment.

What they are saying is, "Look, this is what happens when you try to upset the system and mess with the traditions. We are the guardians of God's law. You should have stayed on the right side of God, like us. This is what happens to people like you who don't play by our rules." Religion can be, and still is, a terrible form of oppression and violence.

Then, second, there is the power of *military force*. The Roman army was an occupying army expressing its power by sheer suppression of all dissent and opposition. So what those Roman soldiers are saying to Jesus is, "Look, this is what happens to terrorist scum like you three up there. We nail you in the end. You don't mess with us. And if some innocent guy gets caught in the middle, well, so much the worse for him. All the better deterrence to the rest of your kind." The way Rome ruled the world by crushing its enemies has had many imitators down the centuries and still today.

Then, third, there's the power of *religious extremist violence.* That was what the criminals on either side of him had exercised (until now, of course). They were probably murderers and bandits. They were probably guerrilla fighters. They believed in and practiced the power of raw violence. And they are saying to Jesus, "See, this is what happens when you don't seize an opportunity like the one you had this week, when you rode into Jerusalem and whipped them out of the temple. You could have led us in a great rebellion against the Romans. We could have drenched the Jordan with their pagan blood. If only you had led us as the real Messiah we wanted. That's the only kind of power the Romans respect: the power of violence and terror." And there are still today those who believe in that kind of ruthless violence for the sake of their religious or political certainties.

But in the midst of all those exhibitions of human power—religious, military, violent (even in defeat)—who is exercising *real* power at this very moment? The answer is, *the powerless one in the middle.* The paradox—the surprise—of this story is that by *choosing* to surrender his life, to give himself up to total powerlessness and weakness, Jesus was actually *exercising* the power of God. Indeed, as Paul will later tell us, it was on the cross that Christ triumphed over all human and satanic powers that opposed God. His power was demonstrated in his powerlessness. The death of Christ in utter weakness would turn out to be the demonstration of the saving power of God that will ultimately destroy all powers of evil and violence. What a paradox! But it lies at the heart of the gospel.

Second, think about the paradox of salvation. All three voices were taunting Jesus to save himself. And the third one that came from the unrepentant criminal was, "Save yourself and us!" "Save *yourself and us.*" But, of course, that was precisely what Jesus could not do. He could not *both* save himself *and* save us. One or the other, but not both.

Of course, Jesus could have saved himself. There's no doubt about that. And Jesus knew it. In fact, at the time of his arrest, Jesus said to his disciples, "Do you think I cannot call on my Father, and he will at once put at my disposal more than twelve legions of angels?" (Mt 26:53). In other words, "I've only got to snap my fingers and a dozen battalions of heaven's hosts will rescue me!" So even at this moment on the cross, as Jesus heard those taunts to save himself, he knew that he could do so at any moment. He could have saved himself the agony. He could have saved himself from death. He could have saved himself from his mockers and torturers. He could have saved himself . . . but if he had done so, then he could not have saved *us.* For it was through his atoning death on our behalf, and by bearing our sins in his own body on the tree, as Peter put it, that we are saved.

So as the insults rang out around his ears, Jesus could do what they all taunted him to do: he could save *himself,* or he could choose to save *us*. But not both. Hadn't he said that the very reason why he had come was "to seek and to save the lost"? In that case, if he was going to save *us*, he could not save *himself*.

And so Jesus *chose not* to save himself. He *chose* to die. He *chose* to stay on the cross for my sake and for your sake; for the sake of those who were crucifying him; for the sake of those he was crucified among. "He was pierced for our transgressions, he was crushed for our iniquities; the punishment that brought us peace was on him, and by his wounds we are healed" (Is 53:5).

You see, by *not* doing what those two criminals *wanted*, he was able to do what they *needed*, which was to provide for them, through his death, a way of salvation—which one of them took.

TWO LAST SAYINGS FULL OF HOPE

We've examined those four scenes that are filled with Scripture. And we've explored those three last temptations that are so full of irony and paradox. Now we need to hear two of the last sayings of Jesus on the cross. One is a prayer in Luke 23:34, and the other is a promise in Luke 23:43. They are both equally surprising, and they're both filled with hope. And it seems to me that, through these two sayings, Luke provides his final lens to help us focus in on his deepest perception of the meaning of the cross of Christ.

The prayer: "Father, forgive them" (Lk 23:34). Even as they are crucifying him, Jesus prays, "Father, forgive them, for they do not know what they are doing."

We are astonished by this, and rightly so. We are astonished because, well, how could *anybody* say this? How could Jesus possibly have such feelings and voice such a prayer for the people who were torturing him with such unbelievably agonizing cruelty at that moment? Who was this man? And what did the soldiers think when they heard him utter such words as they nailed him down and hung him up to die? Well, at least one of them heard, noticed, and drew his own conclusion (Lk 23:47: "Surely this was a righteous man"; compare Mk 15:39: "Surely this man was the Son of God!"). Astonishing indeed.

But it is all the more astonishing because it's quite unprecedented. You see, there is nothing quite like this, even in the Scriptures of the Old Testament that Jesus knew so well. There are a few incidents that point toward it, but they never quite get here. David, for example, showed mercy to a man who had insulted him. But then, just before David died, he told his son Solomon to make sure he took revenge on that man after he, David, was dead (2 Sam 16:5-12; 1 Kings 2:8-9). Hardly a perfect example of forgiving your enemies. Jeremiah wrote to the exiles, surprisingly enough, telling them that they should *pray* for Babylon—their enemies who had destroyed their own city of Jerusalem (Jer 29:7). But even Jeremiah does not tell them to *forgive* the Babylonians.

So what were you supposed to do, or allowed to do, in the Old Testament when people falsely accused you or violently attacked you? First of all, what you were *not* to do was this: you were not to take it upon yourself to avenge the wrong. Violent retaliation was prohibited. "Do not take revenge," says the law of the Old Testament; "that must be left to God. He is the Judge and he will take appropriate action to avenge you if necessary" (see Lev 19:18 and Deut 32:35). So you could not take revenge yourself, but you certainly could ask God to do it for you. And sometimes people did. That is what we find in some of the psalms: people who were being terribly wronged cry out to God to act on their behalf, to punish the wrongdoers and vindicate the innocent. They were simply asking God to do what God had said he would do: namely, do justice by punishing the wicked (only please do it soon).

Jesus would have known very well Old Testament Scriptures like the cry of Isaiah against the wicked people of Jerusalem in his day: "do not forgive them" (Is 2:9). Jesus would have known the cry of Jeremiah when he was suffering persecution, physical beatings, and death threats. Jeremiah prayed: "Bring on them the day of disaster; destroy them with double destruction" (Jer 17:18). Jesus would have known Psalm 69, when the psalmist actually curses his enemies and says, "May they be blotted out" (Ps 69:28). And Jesus would have known about the martyrs during the Maccabean revolt nearly two hundred years before his day. They had fought in a great rebellion against Rome, and some of them, when they were caught and tortured to death, died calling down God's vengeance on their murderers.

But Jesus transcends all that. Jesus, who knew and loved the Old Testament Scriptures, transcends them and prays for his executioners, "Father, forgive them" (Lk 23:34). And in doing so, he sets a whole new standard, a whole new paradigm, of how his followers are to respond to those who hate them and kill them. Jesus was doing and modeling exactly what he had taught his disciples. How shocked they must have been when Jesus said, "Love your enemies . . . bless those who curse you, pray for those who mistreat you" (Lk 6:27-28). But Jesus does just that. He prays for those who are not merely cursing and persecuting him, but are also those who nailed his hands and feet to planks of wood.

And Stephen, who was the first believer in Jesus to be put to death for his faith—the first Christian martyr—followed the example of his Master. Luke tells us that, as they were stoning Stephen to death, he prayed, "Lord, do not hold this sin against them" (Acts 7:60). He was praying for God to forgive his killers.

Can we still do this? Is it possible for Christians to forgive their enemies when they are being violently attacked and killed? Well, it's certainly not possible in human strength alone. The only way we can forgive our enemies is if the living Lord Jesus Christ is formed within us and does it in and through us. Here are two recent examples.

In February 2015, jihadis from the self-described Islamic State murdered twenty-one Coptic Orthodox Christian men, migrant workers from Egypt, by beheading them on a beach in Libya. The news shocked the world and brought intense grief to Egypt, especially to the village where many of the men came from. The mother of victim Tawadros Yousif had this to say about the murderers of her son: "I can't wish them evil. I pray for them that God may open their hearts and give them his light." In a similar vein, Bishop Angaelos of the Coptic Orthodox Church in the United Kingdom commented, "We don't forgive the act because the act is heinous. But we do forgive the killers from the depths of our hearts. Otherwise, we would become consumed by anger and hatred. It becomes a spiral of violence that has no place in this world."

On Christmas Eve 2012, two young men attacked and beat to death Alan Greaves, a sixty-eight-year-old organist who was on his way to church to play for a carol service in London. His widow, Maureen Greaves, with immense courage and struggle, expressed her forgiveness of the two young men, while accepting and approving the justice of their conviction and imprisonment. After the court case, she said this:

Alan was a man who was driven by love and compassion and he would not want any of us to hold on to feelings of hate and unforgiveness. So in honour of Alan and in honour of the God we both love my prayer is that . . . [the killers] will come to understand and experience the love and kindness of the God who made them in his own image and that God's great mercy will inspire them to true repentance.

Coming back to our text: Jesus prays, "Father, forgive them, *for they do not know what they are doing*" (Lk 23:34, emphasis mine). No, indeed, they didn't. For what they were doing, in all its evil brutality, was accomplishing at the human level the deeper will and purpose of God. The cross was a blatant miscarriage of justice and a monstrous evil. But it was no accident. Behind it stood the sovereign will of God that God himself, in the person of his Son, would bear the sin of the world. As Peter put it on the day of Pentecost: "This man was handed over to you by God's deliberate plan and foreknowledge; and you, with the help of wicked men, put him to death by nailing him to the cross" (Acts 2:23).

The crucifixion of Jesus was the wicked act of evil men (in a sense, they knew perfectly well what they were doing and bore responsibility for it); but at the same time it was according to "God's deliberate plan and foreknowledge" (and they certainly had no idea they were involved in that). This is the mystery of how the worst of all evil could be the means by which God accomplished the greatest of all good: the redemption of the world. And so, in putting Jesus to death on the cross, those men were actually carrying out the means by which Jesus' prayer could be answered. Their sin at that very moment was one tiny part of the sin of the world that Jesus would carry on the cross, so that "repentance for the forgiveness of sins will be preached in his name to all nations" (Lk 24:47). Jesus prayed that they *should* be forgiven. And Jesus died so that they *could* be forgiven.

The promise: "today you will be with me in paradise" (Lk 23:43). One of the two condemned terrorists, the same one who had protested against the insults of his friend on the other cross, somehow recognizes the truth about Jesus. This Jesus of Nazareth is indeed God's Messiah. This man on the cross beside him *is* what the inscription over his head says, "The king of the Jews." But more: if he is the Messiah, then he is also God's anointed King who will ultimately reign over Israel and all nations. The kingdom of God *will* come! And Jesus *will* be King!

But that's all future, isn't it? Right now, we're all going to die, aren't we? Obviously! So the kingdom of this Messiah can only happen in the age to come, on resurrection day. Like most other Jews of his day (except the Sadducees), this man would have believed in the day of resurrection. That was the day when all the dead would be raised—the wicked to their just punishment, and the righteous to belong to the people of God in his new kingdom under the rule of the Messiah. Resurrection was for the last day.

Martha, the sister of Lazarus and Mary, believed in the future resurrection of the dead. Lazarus had died, but Jesus said to Martha, "Your brother will rise again." And Martha replies, "I know he will rise again in the resurrection at the last day." It sounds as if she means, "That's all very well, but it's a long time to wait. If you'd got here earlier he needn't have died at all." And then Jesus answers with the astonishing words, in the present tense, "*I am* the resurrection and the life. The one who believes in me will live, even though they die" (Jn 11:23-25, emphasis mine).

That is exactly what is happening in this moment between Jesus and the criminal. He turns to Jesus and says, "Jesus, remember me when you come into your kingdom" (Lk 23:42). *Remember me.* Those are words that have actually been found on tombstones of Jewish people of this era. They are a prayer to God (not just a request to surviving family and friends). What they meant was: "When resurrection day comes, Lord God, when you announce and inaugurate your kingdom, remember *me*, Lord! Don't forget me just because I'm in this tomb! *Remember me* and let me be among the righteous in your kingdom on that final day!" That is probably what the man on the cross beside Jesus meant.

And Jesus surprises him, as he had surprised Martha, by answering in the present tense: "Today!" he says. "Today you will be with me in paradise" (Lk 23:43). Now that doesn't mean, "Today you will go straight to heaven." Even for Jesus that wasn't true. Paradise was not just another word for heaven. That name, in Jewish thought of that time, was used for the intermediate place where the righteous dead were at peace, waiting for the day of resurrection. Jesus was promising that this condemned, crucified man would be among the righteous on that final day. He would share with Jesus in God's kingdom. So he could die this day in peace, "in sure and certain hope of the resurrection" (as it says in *The Book of Common Prayer*), knowing he was among the righteous, the saved—those who would share in the Messiah's reign. In spite of all the sins, wrongdoing, and crimes the man had committed (and which he had just confessed he was guilty of), his future was safe—safe in the hands of Jesus, the Messiah King and Savior, whom he had just acknowledged.

And why was he saved? Because the man confessed his sin, turned to Jesus, and called out to Jesus. He trusted in Jesus, and he was assured of salvation by the promise of Jesus himself (and Luke surely wants his readers, including you and me, to follow that simple example).

The man was saved. Not saved *from* the cross he was on, but eternally saved *through* the cross of the one being crucified beside him. He would die in a few hours. But "the one who believes in me will live, even though they die" (Jn 11:25). And in his very next chapter, Luke will tell the glorious story of Christ's resurrection, when that promise was sealed and guaranteed by God's death-defeating power, and when Christ became the firstfruits of the resurrection of all those who trust in him, including that crucified criminal.

What has Luke given us in his simple yet richly profound description of the crucifixion? Four scenes, three temptations, and two sayings—and through them all (especially the last two sayings), the one whole meaning of what we celebrate at Easter. The answer to Jesus' prayer for forgiveness was only possible through the death of Christ, and the fulfillment of Jesus' promise of eternal life was only possible through the resurrection of Christ.

It will take the rest of the New Testament to explore and explain both of those truths. But for the moment, what Luke has told us in this narrative is all we need to know for them to become a reality for us in our lives today and for our eternal future. Luke has shown us that through Jesus' death on the cross we can have the forgiveness that Jesus prayed for, and that through the resurrection of Christ we can have the future that Jesus promised. Make sure that you have both, for Christ's sake.

CHAPTER FOUR

FROM DARKNESS
TO LIGHT

Mark 15:33–39

At noon, darkness came over the whole land until three in the afternoon. And at three in the afternoon Jesus cried out in a loud voice, "*Eloi, Eloi, lema sabachthani?*" (which means "My God, my God, why have you forsaken me?").

When some of those standing near heard this, they said, "Listen, he's calling Elijah."

Someone ran, filled a sponge with wine vinegar, put it on a staff, and offered it to Jesus to drink. "Now leave him alone. Let's see if Elijah comes to take him down," he said.

With a loud cry, Jesus breathed his last.

The curtain of the temple was torn in two from top to bottom. And when the centurion, who stood there in front of Jesus, saw how he died, he said, "Surely this man was the Son of God!" (Mk 15:33-39)

Mark gives us the shortest and fastest-moving of the Gospels. Indeed, a fifth of his Gospel is taken up describing the final week of Jesus' life on earth, climaxing in his account of the crucifixion itself in chapter 15. And within that, Mark records perhaps the most terrible of all the things that Jesus said during those hours on the cross, words spoken after three hours of darkness: "My God, my God, why have you forsaken me?" (Mk 15:34). That desolate cry came from the depths of the darkness of the cross for Jesus, and yet it signaled the dawning of the light of the gospel for us.

So let us walk with Mark as he takes us into what that awful darkness meant, and then let us walk on with him as he leads us up and out into the light—the light of "the good news about Jesus the Messiah, the Son of God," as he titled his little book (Mk 1:1).

INTO THE DARKNESS

"At noon, darkness came over the whole land until three in the afternoon" (Mk 15:33). Mark actually wrote the hours of the day as they counted them at that time (beginning at dawn). They began the crucifixion of Jesus "at the third hour," which means 9:00 a.m. So the sixth hour was noon, and the ninth hour was 3:00 p.m. For those six hours, Jesus hung on the cross. And in the middle, at noon, the brightest and hottest moment of the day, Luke simply says, "the sun stopped shining" (Lk 23:45). Darkness covered the land. What did that darkness mean? I suggest four possible aspects of that darkness.

Into the cover of darkness. Crucifixion was, quite deliberately, the most unbearably humiliating way to put somebody to death. It was designed by the Romans to inflict maximum shame and mockery. Along with the intense physical pain, the public shame was an added agony. It was the ultimate deterrent. Mark paints this picture very quickly and simply. For his original readers, who lived within the Roman Empire, he didn't need to say anything more than "they crucified him" (Mk 15:24), because everybody knew what that meant. Most people would have seen crucifixions and recoiled from their grisly horror. Men were crucified totally naked, and that helpless exposure in itself was a shameful thing. And then from the shock and the pain of heavy nails crushing and piercing the most sensitive parts of their wrists and feet, victims would be plastered with their own excrement, covered in blood and sweat, and tortured by flies.

Then the jeering and the insults would begin and go on and on, sometimes for days. Mark tells us that's what was happening when they had hoisted Jesus on his cross:

> Those who passed by hurled insults at him, shaking their heads and saying, "So! You who are going to destroy the temple and build it in three days, come down from the cross and save yourself!" In the same way the chief priests and the teachers of the law mocked him among themselves. "He saved others," they said, "but he can't save himself! Let this Messiah, this king of Israel, come down now from the cross, that we may see and believe." Those crucified with him also heaped insults on him. (Mk 15:29-32)

Imagine the noise, shouts, laughter, insults, jeering, and gestures— a raucous roar of mockery around Jesus, rising and subsiding and rising again, for three long hours as the sun rose higher and the day grew hotter . . .

Until God says, "Enough! Enough already, you people! If I am going to hide my face from my only Son, then you will no longer stare at him with your leering laughter and insults." And he switches off the light. The whole scene is drenched in deep and mysterious darkness. I imagine that the noise of the mockery and jeering probably died away and was replaced with a very profound fear, as God took his Son under the cover of darkness.

Into the darkness of creation. Luke simply says, "the sun stopped shining" (Lk 23:45)—as well it might, for its creator was dying. After all, who was this man on that central cross? Let Paul and John remind us.

Paul tells us: "The Son is the image of the invisible God, the firstborn over all creation. For in him all things were created: things in heaven [the sun] and on earth, visible and invisible . . . all things have been created through him and for him" (Col 1:15-16).

And John tells us: "Through him all things were made; without him nothing was made that has been made. In him was life, and that life was the light of all mankind" (Jn 1:3-4).

But now, "the true light that gives light to everyone" (Jn 1:9), Jesus, the uncreated source of the light of the sun itself, was dying. And creation responds. The earth quakes. The sun stops shining. Because on the cross, the Creator himself was bearing the cost of his creation's reconciliation. And creation itself, as it were, goes into mourning and puts on the blackness of cosmic grief.

Into the darkness of judgment. Darkness was a potent symbol for those who knew their Scriptures, which was all those around the cross (except the Roman soldiers). Sometimes in the Gospels, numbers are symbolic, pointing to some significance in the Old Testament Scriptures. For example, Jesus chose twelve disciples, the number of the tribes of Israel. His forty days in the wilderness undoubtedly echo the forty years Israel spent there, being tested through hunger (Deut 8:2-5). And three hours of darkness are reminiscent of the three days of darkness that had been the ninth plague on Egypt, the one before the final plague (the death of the firstborn sons).

> Then the LORD said to Moses, "Stretch out your hand toward the sky so that darkness spreads over Egypt— darkness that can be felt." So Moses stretched out his hand toward the sky, and total darkness covered all Egypt for

three days. No one could see anyone else or move about for three days. (Ex 10:21-23)

God brought a fearful darkness upon the land of Egypt that spoke of his divine anger and judgment against those who were hardening their hearts in refusal to do as he asked. And so, just as darkness spoke then of God's judgment on the Egyptians for what they were doing to God's people Israel, so now darkness at the cross speaks of God's judgment on Israel for what they were doing to God's Messiah, Jesus.

The prophet Amos also speaks of the darkness of God's judgment as a feature of the terrible day of the Lord.

"In that day," declares the Sovereign LORD,

"I will make the sun go down at noon
   and darken the earth in broad daylight. . . .

I will make that time like mourning for an only son
   and the end of it like a bitter day." (Amos 8:9-10)

Darkness at noon was, to those who could hear the echo of Scripture, a clear sign of the judgment of God. But on whom was this darkness of judgment falling? Not just on the crowds. For out of this darkness, and after it had reigned for three hours, comes this terrible cry: "*Eloi, Eloi, lema sabachthani?*' (which means, 'My God, my God, why have you forsaken me?')" (Mk 15:34).

By putting these words of Jesus at exactly this point, Mark tells us that greater even than the physical darkness that had descended on the soldiers, religious leaders, and mocking crowds, was this engulfing darkness of God's judgment that was being borne by the one on the central cross: Jesus himself.

Into the darkness of separation. Here we move, with reverence and awe, into the deepest depth of the mystery and the paradox of the cross. Jesus, who has already borne the physical pain of the flogging and the crucifixion, and the shameful emotional pain of those three long hours of public mockery, now enters the deepest darkness of an infinitely greater suffering—the agony of separation from God his Father. We need to ask two questions about that. First, was it only subjective? And, second, was God really absent?

Was it only subjective? In other words, was it the case that Jesus just *felt* abandoned, because he was in so much pain, but in reality he was not? This is how some people interpret that cry of Jesus. They say: he didn't experience being *actually* separated from God; that was just what it felt like to him. It was a subjective sense of separation, not an objective reality.

But that will not do. That is much too superficial. Such a view doesn't do justice to the terrible depths of the darkness, desolation, and dereliction that Jesus was going through in those three hours of darkness. It doesn't take into account the reality of the burden of sin that Jesus was bearing, and the consequences of doing so.

The Son of God is cut off from his Father. The One who had known perfect communion with his Father from all eternity now loses it. The One who had never known anything but the sunshine, love, and joy of his Father's presence now sinks into the darkness of his Father's absence, cut off and severed from his Father. And he can only cry out, "Why?"

Why indeed? There is only one thing that can separate a human being from God, and that's sin. "Your iniquities have separated you from your God," says Isaiah, "your sins have hidden his face from you, so that he will not hear" (Is 59:2). But Jesus had done no sin.

Even Pontius Pilate acknowledged that Jesus was innocent. Even one of the two terrorists crucified on either side of Jesus acknowledged that. "We are getting what our deeds deserve," he said to the other one. "But this man has done nothing wrong" (Lk 23:41).

So why this terrible cry of separation from his Father? The answer can only be: because it was our sin that he was bearing. It was our sin that cut Jesus off from his Father. "Look," said John the Baptist, "the Lamb of God, who takes away the sin of the world!" (Jn 1:29). And Paul makes it clearest of all: "God made him who had no sin to be sin for us" (2 Cor 5:21).

And so Jesus enters the deepest depths of the darkness of sin itself—the place of God's wrath against sin, the place of God's rejection, abhorrence, and condemnation of all that is evil. Jesus, in those central hours on the cross, goes into that place, in our place. And in that place, he experiences in his humanity the awful, unimaginable reality of separation from God.

"My God, my God, why have you forsaken me?" The words on Jesus' lips are the opening words of Psalm 22. He could have quoted words from Psalm 88 just as truly. Here's another psalmist who expressed the terror of God's wrath, though of course Jesus bore the reality of it in a way the psalmist could never have imagined.

> You have put me in the lowest pit,
>   in the darkest depths.
> Your wrath lies heavily on me;
>   you have overwhelmed me with all your waves. . . .
>
> Why, LORD, do you reject me
>   and hide your face from me? . . .
>
> Your wrath has swept over me;
>   your terrors have destroyed me. . . .
>   darkness is my closest friend. (Ps 88:6-7, 14, 16, 18)

Except that the darkness was no friend at all to Jesus. It was the deepest depth of his suffering.

This is how Donald Macleod, a Scottish theologian, expresses it. I can't put it better than these words:

In the moment of the Son's greatest need and greatest pain, God is not there. The Son cries and is not heard. The familiar resource, the ultimate resource, the only resource, is not there. The God who was always there, the God who was needed now as He had never been needed before, was nowhere to be seen. There was no answer to the Son's cry. There was no comfort. Jesus was left God-less, with no perception of His own Sonship, unable for the one and only time in His life to say, "Abba, Father." He was left with no sense of God's love and no sense of the operation of God's purpose. There was nothing but that "Why?," trying vainly to bridge the Darkness. He was sin. He was lawlessness, and as such He was banished to the Black Hole where lawlessness belongs and from which no sound can escape but, "Why?" That was the Son's only word in His final agony as He reached out to God whom He needed so desperately but whom as Sin He couldn't discern and from whose presence He was outcast. There could be no accord. "God His Son not sparing"! He had to be dealt with not as Son, but as Sin.

In other words, Jesus experienced, in the infinite intensity of being both God and man, what it means to be separated from God. In the mysterious infinity of that time—earthly hours but an eternity in its depth and significance—Jesus experienced what hell is.

In 2 Thessalonians 1:9 Paul outlines the destiny of those who ultimately reject God, who cling to their sin without repentance and refuse to turn to him from their wickedness: "They will be punished with everlasting destruction and shut out from the presence of the Lord." Paul does not use the name, but hell is what he is describing in other terms. Hell is the punishment of eternal destruction, of being cut off from God. Shut out. Separated. Abandoned. And Jesus went to that place.

Some people are tempted to say, "Well, that's okay. If hell is to be separated from God, I can live with that. I mean, I'm doing without God now, so I can do without him forever. What's the difference?" My dear friend, if you're tempted to think like that, please don't. It is nonsense. You may be living *without reference to God* now, but you're certainly not living *without God.* Who do you think is the source of your life, of your health? It is God's creation that gives you the food you eat, the water you drink, and the air you breathe. It is God who is the source of all the love and joy in your relationships, all the exhilaration in your work, your ambitions, your sports, and your recreation. God is the source of all the beauty we enjoy in music, art, and other people's faces, in nature, and in everything! God is the author, giver, and energizing power behind all that makes human life worth living, all that we accomplish with all that God has given. So don't imagine for one moment that your life now is without God.

But do try to imagine what it would be like to be really, actually, totally without God. Imagine being cut off from all of those things which God gives in abundance to make life worth living. No love, no life, no light, no joy, no encouraging relationships— just total and utter aloneness. No peace, no pleasure, no satisfaction, no hope, no silver lining, no future—just the endless absence of everything and anything good, utterly cut off from all that God is, and all that God gives. That is hell. That, perhaps, is the least that hell is.

And Jesus went there. Jesus descended to the depths of that darkness, the outer darkness of separation from God. And Jesus did it so that you and I need never do so. He went there to make it possible for us not to have to go there; so that "whoever believes in him shall not perish but have eternal life" (Jn 3:16). So was that darkness of abandonment just subjective, just something that Jesus felt in himself? No, it was real. It was the most terrifyingly real part of the whole cup of suffering that Jesus drank on the cross.

Was God really absent? Our second question is: Was God really absent from this scene? In other words, as Jesus was dying on the cross and crying out those words, "My God, my God, why have you forsaken me?" was it true that God was not there? Of course, we have to answer again, "No!" And this is the most amazing paradox and mystery of the cross: that God was never more present on earth than at the cross.

"I and the Father are one," Jesus said (Jn 10:30). So that awful sundering, that terrible time of separation, was as much an agony for the Father to impose as it was for the Son to endure. "God," says Paul, "was reconciling the world to himself in Christ" (2 Cor 5:19). The work of our salvation, including this depth of darkness and separation, was the work of God—the whole of God, so to speak. God the Father and God the Son were acting together, as indeed was the Holy Spirit. Hebrews tells us that it was "through the eternal Spirit [that Jesus] offered himself unblemished to God" (Heb 9:14).

God was there on earth as in heaven, on the cross and in the agony of separation, bearing in his own self the cost of our salvation. That was the depth of the darkness of the cross. It was also the beginning of the light.

So, as we move from darkness to light, by way of transition to the second part of our meditation, let's study a poem written by Don Carson. This is a poem that he wrote around these very words of Jesus. Notice how it moves from darkness at the beginning to light at the end.

The darkness fought, compelled the sun to flee,
And like a conquering army swiftly trod
Across the land, blind fear this despot's rod.
The noon-day dark illumined tyranny.
Still worse, abandonment by Deity
Brought black despair more deadly than the blood
That ran off with his life. "My God, my God,"
Cried Jesus, "why have you forsaken me?"
    The silence thundered. Heaven's quiet reigned
    Supreme, a shocking, deafening, haunting swell.
    Because from answering Jesus, God refrained,
    I shall not cry, as he, this cry from hell.
The cry of desolation, black as night,
Shines forth across the world as brilliant light.

INTO THE LIGHT

So now we move *into the light*. Having led us to the darkest moment of the cross, Mark now begins to lead us into the light, which of course will climax in the resurrection.

Into the light of God's creation (Mk 15:33-37). First of all, Mark leads us into the light of God's creation, because he tells us that at the ninth hour (3:00 p.m.) when Jesus died, the darkness that had lasted from the sixth hour (noon) ended.

And the sun came out! The sun that is the symbol in the Bible of the joy of creation shone again. Psalm 19 describes the sun as a joyful athlete running its daily race from one end of heaven to the other.

The sun had risen that Friday morning, only to be darkened at noon as Jesus died. And the sun would rise on Saturday with Jesus still in the tomb. But on the third day, the sun would rise with the rising Son of God himself, bringing about a new creation as the Son of God shone in all his glory. And Paul tells us that all creation in heaven and earth has been reconciled to God through the blood of Christ shed on the cross. So the sun that had refused to shine as Jesus entered the darkness of separation from God came out again as the redemption of the whole creation was beginning.

Into the light of God's victory (Mk 15:34, 37). Second, Mark takes us into the light of God's victory. The cry of Jesus in Mark 15:34 is the first verse of Psalm 22. But when Jesus (or Paul, or any New Testament writer) quotes a verse from the Scripture, it always alludes to the whole context of the quoted verse. And the second half of Psalm 22 goes on to look forward to God's great triumph. Part of that victory is anticipated in verse 27: "All the ends of the earth will remember and turn to the LORD, and all the families of the nations will bow down before him." That is nothing less than God's great promise to Abraham, God's mission to bring blessing to the ends of the earth. Then Psalm 22 ends with the triumphant words, "He has done it!" (Ps 22:31). God will have accomplished it. God will have achieved all that he intended for the salvation of the world. So here is the beginning and the ending of the psalm Jesus quoted. It begins with the terrifying pain of rejection and all the suffering that follows, but it ends with a triumphant affirmation of God's victory.

As we shall see in the final chapter, John tells us that the last words of Jesus on the cross (probably "the loud cry" that Mark refers to in Mark 15:37) was, "It is finished" (Jn 19:30). That means, "It is accomplished!" The victory is won. Jesus has done what he came to do—to bear the sin of the world, to bear the judgment of God, to go to the place of desolate desperation and dereliction for us in our place, and to give his life as a ransom for many. And having achieved that, he could now lay down his life. Jesus died knowing that the light of God's victory was dawning, for he had accomplished it.

Into the light of God's presence (Mk 15:38). Third, Mark takes us into the light of God's presence. In verse 38 he tells us that as Jesus died the curtain of the temple was torn in two from the top to the bottom. That was the curtain that separated the Most Holy Place from the rest of the temple. The Most Holy Place was where God's presence was localized above the ark of the covenant. The thick curtain kept people out from the presence of the glory of the living holy God. Only the high priest could go in there once a year.

So, as Jesus dies, God tears that curtain away from top to bottom, for now there is no longer any barrier. No longer is God shrouded in darkness within a temple. God is now inviting the world into the light of forgiveness and new life through the shed blood of Jesus. Because of the death of Jesus, we are invited into the very presence of God. The cross opens the way. The curtain is torn apart.

And so the writer to the Hebrews, remembering this very event, encourages us to accept that invitation and come right on into the light of God's presence:

> Therefore, brothers and sisters, since we have confidence to enter the Most Holy Place by the blood of Jesus, by a new and living way opened for us through the curtain, that is, his body, and since we have a great priest over the house of God, let us draw near to God with a sincere heart and with the full assurance that faith brings. (Heb 10:19-22)

And isn't it wonderful that in Mark's account of this moment, the very first person through that torn curtain, as it were, the very first person who moved into the presence of God by faith (ignoring for a moment the penitent criminal on the other cross, recorded by Luke), was a Gentile: the Roman centurion who in verse 39 recognizes the truth of what has just happened and walks into the light of faith in the living God!

Into the light of God's Son (Mk 15:39). That brings us finally to our fourth point. Mark takes us into the light of God's Son in verse

39: "And when the centurion, who stood there in front of Jesus, saw how he died, he said, 'Surely this man was the Son of God!'"

The centurion was standing in front of Jesus; that means he was probably the supervising officer. He was in charge of this whole event. And how many other such scenes had he witnessed? How many other people had he crucified? He was probably hardened and ruthless, having done this gruesome job so many times. He must have seen hundreds of people die the same way Jesus was dying, or so he thought. And yet, says Mark, when he heard that cry of Jesus and when he saw how he died, something convinced this pagan centurion of the truth about this man that he had crucified that morning. And so he said, "Surely, this man was the Son of God!"

We may not know how much the centurion understood of the words he had just said, although I'm very happy to believe that it was a genuine saving confession of faith. But Mark, who records the words, understands fully. Indeed, Mark clearly intends us, his readers, to see this as the climax of his whole pulsating Gospel narrative because this title of "Jesus, the Son of God," is like an envelope around his Gospel. He begins and ends on this note. In the very first verse he began, "The beginning of the good news about Jesus the Messiah, *the Son of God*" (Mk 1:1, emphasis mine). And here, close to the end of his Gospel, he records the Roman centurion saying, "Surely this man was *the Son of God*!"

But Mark uses his skill as a writer to make his point even clearer. In Mark 1:10-11, at the baptism of Jesus, Mark says that the heavens were "torn open" and "a voice came from heaven: 'You are my Son.'" And here in Mark 15:38-39, using exactly the same Greek verb (the only two places in the Gospel Mark uses it), he says that when Jesus died on the cross the curtain in the temple was "torn in two," and the centurion's voice spoke: "Surely this is the Son of God."

Two matching occurrences: a tearing and a voice; one the voice of God, the other the voice of a believing human being, both affirming the same thing about Jesus.

So you see, Mark is determined to make sure we know who Jesus is. He is the Son of God. But in Mark's Gospel, up to this point, only God and the demons have ever acknowledged that fact. God declares it twice: first at Jesus' baptism, "You are my Son" (Mk 1:11), and then again at his transfiguration, "This is my Son" (Mk 9:7). The demons called Legion that possessed the Gerasene man declared it after Jesus confronted them, crying out, "What do you want with me, Jesus, Son of the Most High God?" (Mk 5:7).

But in Mark's Gospel, no ordinary human being acknowledges Jesus to be the Son of God—until this moment. I think it's quite deliberate. I think Mark wants us to observe that it was *as he witnessed the death of Jesus* ("when [he] . . . saw how he died," [Mk 15:39]) that this Roman centurion recognized the truth about the man on the central cross. Mark's point is that if we want to truly understand who the Son of God is, we have to see him on the cross. He is the Son who came to give his life. The servant Son. The Son who, willingly doing the will of his Father, chose to bear the cost of our salvation. And in that sense, Mark's purpose is exactly the same as John's. John says at the end of his Gospel: "These [things] are written that you may believe that Jesus is the Messiah, the Son of God, and that by believing you may have life in his name" (Jn 20:31). And Jesus himself says, "whoever hears my word and believes him who sent me has eternal life and will not be judged but has crossed over from death to life" (Jn 5:24). From death to life, from darkness to light.

So what have we got here? We have Mark's stark account of the crucifixion, with hardly a word more than is needed. And yet in it, Mark takes us first into the darkness:

- into the cover of darkness
- into the darkness of creation's mourning
- into the darkness of the judgment of God
- into the outer darkness of the separation between Son and Father for us

But Mark also draws us out of that darkness into the light:

- into the light of the sunshine of a reconciled creation
- into the light of the accomplished victory of God that has been achieved by Christ
- into the light of the presence of God for all who come to him through faith in Jesus
- into the light of the glorious Son of God who died for us

As Paul says, "What, then, shall we say in response to these things? If God is for us, who can be against us? He who did not spare his own Son, but gave him up for us all—how will he not also, along with him, graciously give us all things?" (Rom 8:31-32). God gives us *all things*, including life, forgiveness, and the blessing of an eternity with Christ because Christ went to the place where we need not go if we trust in him.

CHAPTER FIVE

IT IS FINISHED

John 19:28-37

"It is a far, far better thing that I do, than I have ever done; it is a far, far better rest that I go to than I have ever known." Those are the famous last words of the character Sydney Carton in *A Tale of Two Cities*, the well-known novel by Charles Dickens set at the time of the French Revolution. Dickens puts those words into Carton's mind as he climbs the guillotine in Paris to sacrifice his own life, having disguised himself as the man everyone thinks they are executing, Charles Darnay, so that Darnay can escape and go free.

Famous last words of dying heroes are a popular theme in literature and movies. Dickens could write what he liked as the last words of Carton because he was writing fiction, and he was putting these words into the mind and the mouth of his fictional character, one who volunteered to die in the place of another.

John, however, is not writing fiction. Rather, he is inviting us to see the dying moments of the Lord Jesus Christ and to hear some of Jesus' final words in those minutes before his actual death. It seems to me that John shows us the death of Christ from two camera angles, as it were. First, in John 19:28-30, John takes us into the mind of *the one who is experiencing it*, that is, Jesus himself on the cross. And then, in John 19:31-37, John shifts the camera angle to show us the death of Christ through the eyes of *the one who is witnessing it*, namely John himself, the disciple at the foot of the cross.

IN THE MIND OF JESUS

First, then, we view the cross within the consciousness of Jesus.

> Later, knowing that everything had now been finished, and so that Scripture would be fulfilled, Jesus said, "I am thirsty." A jar of wine vinegar was there, so they soaked a sponge in it, put the sponge on a stalk of the hyssop plant, and lifted it to Jesus' lips. When he had received the drink, Jesus said, "It is finished." With that, he bowed his head and gave up his spirit. (Jn 19:28-30)

How did John know what Jesus was thinking at that moment? I can only assume that, after Jesus' resurrection, John asked questions and Jesus explained during the conversations that took place between Jesus and his disciples, including those inner thoughts and intentions that filled his dying moments. So here, as John writes his Gospel, he takes us into the mind of Jesus through one of the things Jesus said and why he said it.

"I am thirsty" (Jn 19:28). Jesus said, "I am thirsty." John must have intended us to see the irony of this. This is the Jesus who had said to the Samaritan woman at the well, "Whoever drinks the water I give them will never thirst" (Jn 4:14). This is the Jesus who had called out in a loud voice at the great Feast of Tabernacles, "Let anyone who is thirsty come to me and drink" (Jn 7:37). This is the

one who declares from the throne of God, "To the thirsty I will give water without cost from the spring of the water of life" (Rev 21:6). And yet Jesus is dying of thirst.

Why did Jesus say these words? The most obvious reason is because they were true. He was desperately thirsty. One of the specific agonies of crucifixion was that it led to excruciating thirst. Dehydration was rapid. There was severe loss of blood caused by the scourging and the nails. There was profuse sweating in reaction to the physical agony. There was exposure to the sun all through the morning past midday. Of course he was thirsty.

But John clearly wants us to see more in these words through the way he describes the moment using three expressions, including Jesus' final words after they gave him some vinegar to drink (Jn 19:28-30). Did you notice the verbs in this passage?

- knowing that everything had now been *finished* (or "accomplished," as translated by many Bibles)
- so that Scripture would be *fulfilled*
- Jesus said, "It is *finished*"

Those three terms—*accomplished*, *fulfilled*, and *finished*—although they are different words in English, are very similar in Greek. In fact, the first and last are exactly the same word: "everything had now been finished . . . Jesus said, 'It is finished.'" And the middle one, "fulfilled," is almost the same word in Greek. They all have the sense of a purpose being achieved and completed.

John wants us to realize that in the consciousness of Jesus at this point, the whole experience is one of *achievement*. That's the amazing paradox. In his dying moments, the mind of Jesus is filled, not with hopeless despair, but with a sense of accomplishment. His imminent death was not merely something others had inflicted on him, but something he himself had achieved!

John tells us that Jesus spoke those words, "I am thirsty," for two reasons: (1) because of what he *knew* (that all things were now accomplished), and (2) because of what he *intended* (so that the Scripture should also be accomplished). In other words, this was the totally deliberate word and action of a man who, even though he was at the point of death, was still in total control of himself, his thoughts, his intentions, his words, and his actions. Let's look at these three key phrases in these verses as John gives them to us.

Everything had now been finished (Jn 19:28). Jesus was not actually dead yet, but he was triumphantly conscious that nothing could now stand in the way of his death. This was what he had come to do. This was what his Father had sent him for. The whole plan of God that stretched back to eternity before Jesus' birth in time was now coming to completion. His life's goal was to give his life as a ransom for many. That was God's will and his own will, and now he'd reached the point of no return. He was, as we might say, around the last bend and into the finishing straightaway. There was nothing that could stop that moment when he would give his life. His death was now inevitable.

But, we might ask, what was the point of thinking that? Surely Jesus didn't have much choice! There he was, stretched out on the cross. How could he be thinking, "That's it! I've done it! Made it at last!"? Well, that is actually the point. It was only because Jesus had been so utterly *determined* to die that he had reached this point of no return.

If you think about it, almost everybody had tried to stop Jesus from getting to this place of giving his life. Right at the start, Herod tried to put him to death when he was a little baby. The whole story could have stopped right there. And then, when Jesus entered his ministry, the devil tried to tempt Jesus not to go the way of obedience to his Father, which would lead to suffering and death, offering him much more attractive alternatives. At Caesarea Philippi, when Jesus began to explain to his disciples what lay ahead, Peter said, "No, no, Lord, that's not going to happen to you!" Later on, his own mother and family tried to pull him back from his mission that was clearly offensive and dangerous. In Jesus' own worst moment at Gethsemane, from within his own battling human consciousness, had come this deep, deep longing not to have to drink the cup that his Father was giving him. When they arrested him, he knew he could have called on squadrons of angels to rescue him. And earlier that very morning Pilate had tried to release him. Even in those early moments on the cross, the criminals on either side of him had urged him (with mockery, of course), "Save yourself and us!" (which he could have done). So it was only because Jesus had been determined to go the whole way to death that he had reached this final point of victory. Everything was now finished. All was completed. Nothing more stood in the way of Jesus giving his life and finishing the task for which his Father had sent him.

So that Scripture would be fulfilled (Jn 19:28). The Scriptures that had guided Jesus all the way through his life now filled even his dying consciousness. Five days earlier and seven chapters before in John's Gospel, on what we now call Palm Sunday, Jesus had ridden into Jerusalem on a donkey, and there too John tells us that it was to fulfill Scripture, namely (on that occasion) Zechariah 9:9. John also tells us that it was only after the resurrection that the disciples understood all this, which is why I suggested that John got his insight into the motivation of Jesus' words on the cross from the risen Jesus himself. And so here, with Scripture in mind, Jesus says, "I thirst."

Which Scripture, we might ask? Well, as we saw in chapter 3, it could have been Psalm 69:21: "They . . . gave me vinegar for my thirst." That is the verse that Luke probably saw reflected in his account of the vinegar-soaked sponge. But I think John almost certainly means that the Scripture Jesus himself had in mind was Psalm 22:15: "My mouth is dried up like a potsherd [a piece of broken pottery], and my tongue sticks to the roof of my mouth [that's thirst!]; you lay me in the dust of death."

That is most likely the verse that Jesus is thinking of, since we know from Mark that Jesus had quoted Psalm 22:1 when he cried out at the climax of his sufferings, "My God, my God, why have you forsaken me?" And John has himself already quoted from Psalm 22:18, when he describes how the soldiers divided up Jesus' clothes among themselves by casting lots (Jn 19:23-24).

What is it that Jesus finds in Psalm 22 that so fills his mind? I think he is actually taking both halves of the psalm to himself. Look at the first half of the psalm up to verse 21. It is the cry of someone going through acute suffering, someone who feels abandoned by God and abused by people, someone who describes his suffering in a series of violent metaphors: attacked by dangerous animals, paralyzed, pierced, speechless, defenseless, stripped naked, exposed, trapped, pinned down. It is a terrifying portrayal, and some of the images the psalmist used to describe his suffering became literally true for Jesus in his crucifixion. So Jesus could certainly identify with the first half of Psalm 22 and see his own suffering as its fulfillment.

But the second half of Psalm 22 (from verse 22 to the end), amazingly and without explanation, goes on to anticipate praising God for salvation. The psalmist expects not only that God will deliver and vindicate him, but also that God's salvation will extend to the poor (v. 26), and the rich (v. 29), to generations that have died (v. 29), and to generations yet to come (v. 30). Indeed, God's salvation will be so comprehensive that:

All the ends of the earth
    will remember and turn to the LORD,
and all the families of the nations
    will bow down before him,
for dominion belongs to the LORD
    and he rules over the nations. (Ps 22:27-28)

So, when Jesus declared his thirst "so that Scripture would be fulfilled," he was not just ticking off one more little box on a list of Bible predictions. No, Jesus saw a profound resonance with what was happening to him at that moment and the message and vision of Psalm 22 *as a whole*. Jesus found *in both halves* of the psalm words that expressed *both* the depths of his suffering *and* the breadth of his faith and his hope. And so the Scriptures that had governed his every living moment continued to govern even his dying breath.

"It is finished" (Jn 19:30). Jesus' final words in John's account probably echo the final words of Psalm 22, which, as we have just seen, was filling Jesus' mind at that moment. At the climax of his song, the psalmist says that all the great things he anticipates *will* happen because God himself will accomplish them. Future generations will praise God: "They will proclaim his righteousness, declaring to a people yet unborn: He has done it!" (Ps 22:31).

That is what Jesus now celebrates with his dying breath. John emphasizes the meaning through his use of the three phrases in John 19:28-30; all things have now been completed, the Scripture has been fulfilled, and it is now accomplished. God has done it!

We might ask: what exactly has been accomplished? To answer that question we need more Scriptures than those quoted by Jesus and John here; we need Scriptures that explain the whole plan and purpose of God. Let's examine a few Scriptures that will help us to fill out the full meaning of what God accomplished through the cross of Christ.

It was the plan of God to deal with all the guilt of human sin in order for God's own justice to be vindicated. And at the cross, God accomplished that by taking that guilt and punishment upon himself in the person of his own Son Jesus Christ. "The Lord . . . laid on him the iniquity of us all" (Is 53:6), when "'He himself bore our sins' in his body on the cross" (1 Pet 2:24).

It was the plan of God to defeat all the powers of evil and all the demonic forces that crush, invade, and destroy human life. And at the cross, God accomplished that when Christ "disarmed the powers and authorities . . . triumphing over them by the cross" (Col 2:15).

It was the plan of God to destroy death, the great invader and enemy of human life in God's world. And at the cross, God accomplished that when by Christ's death he destroyed the one "who holds the power of death—that is, the devil" (Heb 2:14), and "destroyed death and . . . brought life and immortality to light through the gospel" (2 Tim 1:10).

It was the plan of God to remove the barrier and the alienation between Jews and Gentiles and ultimately to remove all forms of enmity and hatred between human beings. And at the cross, God accomplished that through Christ: "For he himself is our peace, who has made the two groups one and has destroyed the barrier, the dividing wall of hostility. . . . His purpose was to create in himself one new humanity out of the two, thus making peace, and in one body to reconcile both of them to God through the cross, by which he put to death their hostility" (Eph 2:14-16).

It was the plan of God ultimately to heal and reconcile his whole creation—the great cosmic mission of God. And at the cross of Christ, God accomplished that in anticipation. For it is God's will "through [Christ] to reconcile to himself all things, whether things on earth or things in heaven, by making peace through his blood, shed on the cross" (Col 1:20).

That's some catalog of accomplishments! Did you grasp it? Let me summarize it again. God's ultimate will, plan, and purpose was:

- that sin should be punished and sinners forgiven

- that evil should be defeated and humanity liberated

- that death should be destroyed, and life and immorality brought to light

- that enemies should be reconciled to one another and to God

- that the whole of creation should be restored and reconciled to its creator

And all of that was accomplished at the cross, and was then affirmed, vindicated, and guaranteed by the resurrection. All that God intended has now been accomplished. *"It is finished."*

That was one single word in the original language as Jesus spoke it. And on that one word hangs the uniqueness of the Christian message. Because it is the Christian gospel alone which says that salvation is not a matter of *what you can do* to please God and deserve his favor; no, it is *what God has already done* to save you and his whole world.

And on that one word also hangs the whole basis of the Christian's personal assurance. When I contemplate the cross, I have to remind myself that I am included in the sin that put Jesus there. But at the same time, I must see myself included in the complete atonement that he accomplished there. Jesus dealt with sin. All sin. My sin. Jesus said, "It is finished!" So it's not for me to turn around and say, "Oh no it isn't. There are things I need to do as well." We fall into the habit of thinking we must do this and that to pay for our sins, especially when life isn't going well and we think God is somehow still punishing us. Sometimes I find myself coming into the presence of God in prayer with this thought in my head: "Lord, I don't really deserve you to listen and answer my prayers today because I haven't been a particularly good Christian recently . . . I feel ashamed and guilty." But then I need to tell myself very forcefully, "I never *deserved* God to answer my prayers, ever!" It's not a matter of deserving, but of receiving what God has accomplished by his love and grace. Of course it is right to confess our sin and be ashamed of it, but only with the intention of remembering once again that it has been fully borne by Jesus on the cross and that I can be assured of peace with God and a clean conscience.

I think John records these words of Jesus in order to say to us, "Listen to what Jesus said, will you? Jesus said, 'It is finished.' Believe him and be assured of forgiveness and eternal life!" *All* the guilt of *all* the sin of *all* my life was borne by Christ. As one old hymn puts it:

> My sin, oh, the bliss of this glorious thought!
> My sin, not in part but the whole,
> Is nailed to the cross, and I bear it no more;
> Praise the Lord, praise the Lord, O my soul!

And as a more recent hymn has put it:

> It was my sin that held Him there
> Until it was accomplished;
> His dying breath has brought me life–
> I know that it is finished.

Do *you* know that? I hope so.

He gave up his spirit (Jn 19:30). John makes one last observation about the inner consciousness of Jesus: "With that, he bowed his head and gave up his spirit." That is quite deliberate language. John means that Jesus did not just expire. He did not just lose consciousness. He did not even just *lose* his life. Jesus *gave up* his life. This was his moment, it was his active choice, and he was conscious of making that choice, finishing the task he had come to do. In fact, Jesus had said so earlier: "The reason my Father loves me is that I lay down my life—only to take it up again. *No one takes it from me, but I lay it down of my own accord.* I have authority to lay it down and authority to take it up again. This command I received from my Father" (Jn 10:17-18, emphasis mine). So, at this moment, Jesus chooses (as he had done all his life) to do the will of his Father, and deliberately gives up his life in death.

His inner awareness (at the beginning of John 19:28) that "everything had now been finished" means that the will of God the Father has been accomplished. And his final act, in which "he gave up his spirit" (at the end of John 19:30), means that the will of God the Son has now been accomplished. There is here perfect harmony between the Father and the Son in the death of Jesus, just as there had been all through his life. And this is actually a very important theological point.

There are some people who don't like the idea of Jesus dying in our place, the idea that he took the punishment we deserve. They feel that what the Bible portrays as the ultimate act of God's justice is somehow actually unfair and unjust. This is because they imagine that God in his anger was making Jesus the whipping boy for everything we deserve. They then caricature that as if God were like an abusive father victimizing his son for something he did not do, so that a guilty party escapes. Such a view of the atonement has even been mocked as "cosmic child abuse." The main trouble with this distortion is that it sees the atonement as a drama with *three* actors: A (an angry God), B (sinful humanity), and C (Jesus). So A ought to punish B, but instead A puts C in B's place and punishes him instead—which is irrational and unjust. But this overlooks the essential unity of Father and Son (which Jesus has stressed all through John's Gospel). The atonement drama has only two actors: the one triune God and us. And it is God who bears *in himself* the consequences of our sin. God puts *himself* in our place on the cross. He does not "punish somebody else instead." It was God's self-substitution in our place through his own Son. "God was reconciling the world to himself in Christ" (2 Cor 5:19). The Bible sometimes expresses this with balancing statements, and we need to take both sides of the balance seriously.

So, for example, we know that the cross was *God's* will (Acts 2:23). Yes, but Jesus also said, "*My food [will]* is to do the will of him who sent me" (Jn 4:34, emphasis mine).

Isaiah 53:6 says that "the LORD has laid on him the iniquity of us all." Yes, but Peter also adds, "'He himself bore our sins' in his body on the cross" (1 Pet 2:24).

John tells us that "God so loved the world that *he gave* his one and only Son" (Jn 3:16, emphasis mine). Yes, but Paul adds, "The Son of God . . . loved me and *gave himself* for me" (Gal 2:20, emphasis mine). The Father's plan and the Son's actions go together in perfect harmony.

The book *The Cross of Christ* by John Stott is a classic. In one section, he discusses exactly this point, and he said it far better than I can:

> We have no liberty . . . to imply either that God compelled Jesus to do what he was unwilling to do himself, or that Jesus was an unwilling victim of God's harsh justice. Jesus Christ did indeed bear the penalty of our sins, but God was active in and through Christ doing it, and Christ was freely playing his part (e.g. Heb 10:5-10).

We must not, then, speak of God punishing Jesus or Jesus persuading God, for to do so is to set them over against each other as if they acted independently of each other or in conflict with each other. We must never make Christ the object of God's punishment or God the object of Christ's persuasion, for both God and Christ were subjects not objects, taking the initiative together to save sinners. Whatever happened on the cross in terms of "God-forsakeness" was voluntarily accepted by both in the same holy love which made atonement necessary.... The Father did not lay on the Son an ordeal he was reluctant to bear, nor did the Son extract from the Father a salvation he was reluctant to bestow. There is no suspicion anywhere in the New Testament of discord between the Father and the Son.... There was no unwillingness in either. On the contrary, their wills coincided in the perfect self-sacrifice of love.

Never separate the Father and the Son in your understanding of the cross. They were as one in Christ's death as they were one in his life.

THROUGH THE EYES OF JOHN

So John has taken us in those dying moments of Jesus into the consciousness of Jesus himself. We move on in John 19:31-37 to see the scene through the eyes of John, who was standing close by at the foot of the cross. Jesus has bowed his head in death in verse 30, but John witnesses one more act in this drama—an act which then leads him to recall and quote two more Scriptures (as if he hadn't already recalled enough for us!).

Now it was the day of Preparation, and the next day was to be a special Sabbath. Because the Jewish leaders did not want the bodies left on the crosses during the Sabbath, they asked Pilate to have the legs broken and the bodies taken down. The soldiers therefore came and broke the legs of the first man who had been crucified with Jesus, and then those of the other. But when they came to Jesus and found that he was already dead, they did not break his legs. Instead, one of the soldiers pierced Jesus' side with a spear, bringing a sudden flow of blood and water. The man who saw it has given testimony, and his testimony is true. He knows that he tells the truth, and he testifies so that you also may believe. These things happened so that the scripture would be fulfilled: "Not one of his bones will be broken," and, as another scripture says, "They will look on the one they have pierced." (Jn 19:31-37)

Once again, John perceives some sharp ironies in the way he describes this moment. The Jewish leaders were concerned about the Sabbath, when the Lord of the Sabbath himself was dying. Those leaders were concerned not to pollute or desecrate the land by having death and blood on it (that's the theology that lies behind their request), when the Creator himself was shedding his blood for the redemption of the whole earth.

Those leaders were concerned about the curse of having a dead body hanging from a tree overnight (Deut 21:22-23), when Jesus was dying under God's curse in order to lift that curse from the earth and from us forever. Or perhaps those leaders were just eager to get ready for the Passover and to kill the Passover lambs, when the Passover Lamb of God had already shed his blood.

So they ask for his legs to be broken. The reason for that was to hasten death. Once the legs of a crucified man were broken, he could no longer push himself up to get some breath. So, hanging only from his extended arms, he would die much sooner from as-phyxia. The soldiers spring into action with their heavy iron mallet to smash the legs of the other two criminals. But when they reach Jesus they find, surprisingly, that he's already dead. As John has already told us, Jesus gave up his spirit. Nobody took his life from him; he gave it up himself.

So one of the soldiers stabs him with his long spear, just to make sure Jesus is dead. He stabs through Jesus' side from below. The puncture of the chest cavity through the diaphragm releases the red blood cells and the clear serum that had separated through the internal bleeding caused hours before by the flogging and the damage to his chest and organs. So the spear thrust releases a gush of blood and water.

And John was there, watching, witnessing, and in John 19:35 he testifies to what he saw as an eyewitness of Jesus' death. For the mere facts proclaim that Jesus was indeed unquestionably dead, as confirmed by John, by the soldiers (who knew when a man was dead or not), and by the evidence of the separated blood and water. Jesus had not just fainted (and then later revived in the coolness of the tomb, as one of the more crazy explanations of the resurrection would have it). Jesus was dead. He was no longer struggling for breath. There was no need to break his legs.

People see various symbolic meanings in the water and the blood. For example, water was a means of cleansing; blood, the means of atoning. Or we might think of the poetry of August Toplady's hymn, "Rock of Ages," with its lines,

> Let the water and the blood,
> From Thy riven side which flowed,
> Be of sin the double cure,
> Cleanse me from its guilt and power.

But we should stick to the text and listen to John himself. For he tells us explicitly that the soldiers' actions (*not* breaking Jesus' legs, but piercing his side instead) reminded him of two more Scriptures. And so we need to turn to those two Scriptures, finally, to see Jesus' last moments on the cross through the double lens that John provides for us.

His bones were not broken. John records, first of all, that Jesus' bones were not broken. And that reminds him of a small detail in the narrative of the exodus and Passover. God's instructions about the Passover lamb include the detail, "Do not break any of the bones" (Ex 12:46). We thought about the meaning of the Passover in chapter 1. It celebrated how, when God was bringing his final plague on the Egyptians—the slaying of their firstborn sons—the Israelites were spared, protected by the blood of a Passover lamb smeared on their doorposts. The annual Passover festival remembered and celebrated that great moment in the exodus story.

And so John watches Jesus die outside the city wall, at the very time when the Passover lambs are being slaughtered inside the city of Jerusalem. The people are preparing to celebrate God's great deliverance of his people from slavery. And John's mind connects with that Scripture about the Passover lamb. He remembers how John the Baptist had pointed to Jesus as the Lamb of God who takes away, not just the slavery of his own people, but indeed the sin of the whole world (Jn 1:29, 36). And now, here at the cross, John sees that this is the moment of redemption that surpasses even the exodus. Christ's death, then, is the sacrifice for our sins that has brought us life and salvation. His death is that "full, perfect, and sufficient sacrifice, oblation, and satisfaction for the sins of the whole world." Here is the true Passover Lamb, slain for our salvation. Here is the Lamb who will stand in the center of God's throne surrounded by all the company of heaven, who sing,

You are worthy to take the scroll
      and to open its seals,
because you were slain,
      and with your blood you purchased for God
      persons from every tribe and language and people
            and nation.

You have made them to be a kingdom and priests to serve
            our God,
      and they will reign on the earth. . . .

Worthy is the Lamb, who was slain,
      to receive power and wealth and wisdom and strength
      and honor and glory and praise! . . .

To him who sits on the throne and to the Lamb
      be praise and honor and glory and power,
      for ever and ever! (Rev 5:9-13)

And John says, "I was there. I saw it. I heard him cry, 'It is finished!' I saw him bow his head and give up his spirit. I saw the blood and water that flowed from his side. But I also saw that not one of his bones was broken. And I tell you, he is the Passover Lamb of God. I want you to see what I saw. I want you to hear what I heard. And I want you to believe what I believe, so that in believing in Jesus you may have eternal life in his name" (see Jn 20:31).

His side was pierced. So not a bone was broken, but his side was pierced. And that reminds John of another text from the prophet Zechariah. God said to Israel:

> I will pour out on the house of David and the inhabitants of Jerusalem a spirit of grace and supplication. They will look on me, the one they have pierced, and they will mourn for him as one mourns for an only child, and grieve bitterly for

him as one grieves for a firstborn son. . . . On that day a fountain will be opened to the house of David and the inhabitants of Jerusalem, to cleanse them from sin and impurity. (Zech 12:10; 13:1)

God had said that the sins of Israel had pierced him (i.e. God). God felt that Israel had stabbed him with their evil ways. It is a vivid metaphor; God himself wounded and hurt by the sins of his people. But God promises that he will give to them such a spirit of grace that when they look on him whom they have pierced (i.e. God) they will mourn and grieve for what they have done. This, then, is a moment of repentance, which is immediately followed by the promise of forgiveness, cleansing, and healing. And that, I think, is how John intends us to interpret the prophecy in the light of what he has just witnessed at the cross: God himself, in the person of Jesus Christ, being pierced; the casual spear-thrust of a Roman soldier portraying all that human sin and evil have done to our Lord and God and Creator. That is the text in Zechariah that John quotes. But Revelation extends it in similar language:

"Look, he is coming with the clouds,"
 and "every eye will see him,
even those who pierced him";
 and all peoples on earth "will mourn because of him."
(Rev 1:7)

That text inspired Charles Wesley's great Advent hymn, "Lo! He Comes with Clouds Descending." I don't know about you, but I always find it impossible to sing the second verse of that hymn:

Every eye shall now behold him,
Robed in dreadful majesty;
Those who set at naught and sold him,

Pierced and nailed him to the tree,
Deeply wailing, deeply wailing, deeply wailing,
Shall their true Messiah see.

I find that verse troublesome, first, because it just seems too horrible to *sing* about such a prospect. But it is also troublesome, second, because it seems to suggest that only the Jews who actually crucified Jesus will wail in remorse because they will recognize Jesus too late. It reinforces the prejudice that the Jews are to blame for Christ's death, and one day they will realize the truth when it's too late to repent. That kind of thinking seems to go way beyond what John sees at this moment.

For when we consider the context of the quotation from Zechariah, it is likely that John intends the Scripture to be heard as a prayer and a hope that those who were, in a direct sense, the *cause* of Christ's death would come to mourn in repentance and be *saved* by Christ's death. That is what John is longing for in writing his whole Gospel. And indeed, in his very next verses he points to some among the Jewish leaders who responded to Jesus very differently from those who condemned him to death. In John 19:38-42 we meet Joseph of Arimathea and Nicodemus, who act in love and faithfulness toward Jesus. They did indeed look on him, and they mourned and grieved for his death; but they did so in faith, and their faith was rewarded by his resurrection.

But, finally, *who* pierced and nailed him to the tree? Can we blame only the Jews who condemned him and the Romans who crucified him? Of course not.

He was pierced for *our* transgressions,
        he was crushed for *our* iniquities;
    the punishment that brought us peace was on him,
        and by his wounds *we* are healed. (Is 53:5, emphasis mine)

It was my sin that held him there. It was your sin that held him there. And John says, "Look at him. Look at him and mourn. But let that mourning be the mourning of repentance that brings you to faith in Christ and eternal life through him."

John's portrait of the suffering and death of Jesus Christ is now complete. He has taken us right into the consciousness of the dying Jesus and shown us that Jesus knew that his death was not a failure and defeat, but rather the greatest achievement in history, fulfilling the plan of God for the whole of creation. And then John has put us in the place of an eyewitness, enabling us to see what he saw. And as we see the scene through John's eyes, we also see it through the lens of Scripture that he holds up. He tells us to understand the death of Jesus as God's own sacrifice, the self-sacrifice of the Lamb of God taking upon himself the sin of the world, so that we might have life and salvation.

He was lifted up to die;
"It is finished!" was his cry;
Now in heaven exalted high:
Hallelujah, what a Savior!

PREPARING
TO PROCLAIM

For those fellow pilgrims on the adventure of Bible preaching, I thought it might be helpful to add some personal reflections on how I went about the task of preparing to preach the sermons that fill the preceding five chapters (insofar as I can remember!). I will begin with some general comments, and then move on to specific comments relevant to each sermon.

GENERAL COMMENTS

The All Souls context. Each of the five sermons was preached at All Souls Church, Langham Place, in the season of Easter in different years. That fact is relevant for several reasons.

First, the biblical texts were assigned to me, not chosen by myself. I am part of the preaching team at All Souls, but the planning of sermon series and the choice of texts in relation to each sermon in a series is the responsibility of the rector (first Richard Bewes and then Hugh Palmer). It is possible that if the choice of

text had been my own, I might have chosen a different or sometimes shorter selection of verses from the relevant chapters in each
of the four Gospels. Sometimes one is given a passage that feels
too long for a single sermon. Nevertheless, it is a very useful and
challenging discipline to be asked to preach on a given text. It
forces you to set about the task of studying that whole passage
carefully and without complaint!

Second, sermons at All Souls are usually around thirty to thirty-
five minutes in length, and the congregation expects that. So if the
sermons you read in these chapters felt perhaps a bit longer and
heavier than you would expect to preach in your own church, please
understand the context of the originals! In some cases, the material
could be broken up into several separate sermons over a few weeks.

Third, the majority of those who gather in the regular congrega-
tions that meet at All Souls are already Christian believers, though
from a wide range of nationalities and cultures. We are always
aware that there will be non-Christians in the congregation, some
brought as guests by church members, others simply curious vis-
itors. So in our preaching we try to include an element of evangelistic challenge and invitation. However, the regular expository
Bible preaching ministry at All Souls is not *primarily* evangelistic
(except at designated guest services or similar events). There is a
stronger emphasis on teaching and nurturing believers in their
faith, deepening their understanding of the Bible, and, by relevant
application, encouraging and equipping them for mission in the
world. Accordingly, in these sermons of mine about the cross, in-
evitably the evangelistic appeal of the gospel shines through, I
hope; but the main aim was to lead believers into a deeper understanding of the love and grace of God poured out at Calvary. My
aim was to help them appreciate how the Gospel writers portray
that event with such simplicity, and yet with so many echoes of the

Old Testament Scriptures. For it is the Scriptures that provided the lenses through which they saw and interpreted what they described.

My own preparation. As for all my biblical sermons, the work started with careful reading of the whole Bible text, along with its wider context, many times over. I usually try to do this with a few different English translations, and normally I read the passage in my Greek New Testament as well. When Bible passages are very familiar to us, as the stories of the suffering and death of Jesus undoubtedly are, it is important not just to skim along thinking, "I've read all this before." The work of reading the Greek (if you are able to do that, of course!) forces you to think about the different ways it has been translated into your own language, and consider what reasons there may be for any variations.

I sometimes try to read a text imagining that I am reading it for the very first time, wondering what would strike me as surprising, or unusual, or needing explanation. And in this early reading and re-reading, I have a constant prayer in my mind, asking God through the Holy Spirit to show me what he wants me to see in this text, to hear what he wants me to hear, and to know what he wants me to say when I eventually come to preach it.

In the Bible I use for such study, I freely underline repeated words, draw lines making connections that I observe, jot notes in the margins, and so on. And I have a sermon preparation notebook in which I keep notes of any longer observations during that reading stage. My sermon preparation notebooks (I have many that are used up over the years) are small and thin so that I can carry them with me easily, along with my Bible, if I am traveling in the weeks before preaching and keep jotting things in there while they are fresh in my mind.

In all that early study of the passage I try to discern the inner structure of the text, the main point that the author is driving at, and any obvious patterns, contrasts, comparisons, or conclusions. I find that a lot of the hard work of sermon preparation lies at this stage of simply chewing over the text again and again, trying to see into it and underneath it.

With New Testament passages, and especially in the Gospels, there will almost always be echoes of Old Testament Scriptures. Some of these I can spot immediately (especially if the writer is kind enough actually to say what he is quoting!); others are found in the cross-reference notes of my Bible. So another preparation task is to read those Old Testament passages too, and see why the Gospel writer has quoted or alluded to them. What was in his mind? How does the lens of that Scripture affect the way the writer wants us to see the event he is describing or the words that one of the characters in the Gospel story speaks? As I discover and make notes on these Old Testament background texts, I will also be trying to decide whether *in my sermon* I will want to refer to them and explain them, so that the congregation hears the full resonance of the New Testament text—or whether that would be too distracting or be too much detail to include in one sermon. That is never an easy judgment to make, but we do have to be disciplined. Remember that we simply cannot include in one sermon everything we may discover about a particular passage in the course of our study of it. We need to select what will be the most helpful for people to understand and remember.

At some stage in that study of the Bible passage I will begin to jot down ideas for a sermon outline structure, a few short headings or points, clustered around what I think will be the main point of the passage, which I also want to be the main point of my sermon. This may go through many modifications as new ideas occur. Basically, I am aiming for something that is short (not too many headings, and only a few words in each) and easy to remember.

Then I turn to any commentaries I have on that book of the Bible. Some of us are blessed with having many, some of us have only a few, and some may perhaps have only one or a one-volume commentary on the whole Bible. But the quantity doesn't matter. It's what you do with what you have that counts. And what you *shouldn't* do is try to get everything you read in the commentaries into your sermon! Reading commentaries can be very fascinating, and they will tell you things you did not previously know, for example, about the background or culture of the book. But what you have to decide about every item of information you discover is: Is it, *or is it not*, relevant to the main points you want to get across in your sermon? Again, it is a matter of discipline and selection. Whatever is truly helpful can be worked in. Whatever is merely fascinating should be left aside. People can put lots of different things into a book, but you must stick to your main aim in each sermon.

As I read my commentaries on the passage I take notes in my sermon notebook; these are usually very rough notes, with a heading of the name of the commentary writer and the page numbers so that I can go back and refer again if I need to, or if I want to quote something in the sermon itself. When I have finished as much reading as I can, I sit back, read the Bible text again, and then skim through all my notes to see if any stand out as really deserving some input into the sermon itself, and I mark those with a red asterisk so I don't lose sight of them later. But, as I mentioned above, a lot of what I may have jotted down as rough notes (because I found them interesting) will never be included in the sermon, but they will still have been helpful in my own deeper understanding of the passage.

Then comes the hardest bit (I find, anyway): working out an outline for the sermon. This involves more prayer, talking through the ideas in my mind with the Lord and asking for his help to make this part of his Word clear to me and, through me, to those who will listen to the sermon. Often this stage involves a lot of walking around for me! I find that pacing up and down helps me put my thoughts into order. If I am on my own, I often talk out loud as I think, which again helps me to clarify the ideas (if they sound crazy, they probably are crazy!). Bit by bit a shape emerges, points get clearer, headings turn up, and I jot those things down in outline. That part of the preparation is often the longest and scariest part. Somehow, the more you've thought and read around a passage, the more the thought keeps cropping up, "How on earth am I going to preach this? How can I 'capture' all this in a sermon? What will be my central point, and how can I make it all hang together?" It's never easy, but when the Lord begins to answer your desperate prayers and some structure does begin to take shape, it is very satisfying because it is probably the most creative part of the process.

I then usually scribble a draft version of the sermon in rough notes (in my little sermon preparation notebook). If possible, I leave it there for a few days before writing up the final clear version that I will preach from. That final version goes on loose-leaf lined paper for my preaching notebook, which sits very comfortably beside my Bible in a pulpit or on a lectern.

I know that many people now preach from typed notes or from tablet screens. I personally find that my own handwritten notes serve me best in the actual act of preaching itself. I don't know why that is so; it may be something to do with the links between my own hand, my eyes, my brain, and my mouth! My sermon notes are fairly full. It is not a word-for-word script that I simply read aloud; but neither is it merely headings to be filled in out of my head as I'm actually preaching. I like to have clear notes of what I have prepared to say so that I don't get lost but with enough freedom to be able to expand or emphasize here and there in the sermon itself, knowing that God the Holy Spirit will usually have more to say than I may have prepared in advance, and I am open to that.

In Langham Preaching seminars I often tell people that, when you preach, there are three people in the pulpit (two really present, and one in imagination). There is you, of course. You are the one who is visible, the one people are watching and hearing. You are the one who has done all the hard work of preparation and have a message that you have prayed over. So speak clearly, confidently, and humbly. Second, there is the Holy Spirit. I think of him as being behind my left shoulder. He is the author of the Word you are preaching. He caused it to be written, translated, copied, printed, and available now to his people, and he wants to speak to people's hearts through his Word via your words. What a responsibility and privilege! And third, there is the original writer of the Bible passage you are preaching. I imagine him as being behind my right shoulder. I like to hope that as he listens to my preaching he is nodding in approval, agreeing that what I am saying is (more or less) what he wanted to say. (At least, I hope he is not shaking his head in despair, thinking, "No, no, no! That's not what I meant at all! Be quiet and sit down!")

That leaves only one small final act of preparation that comes immediately before I preach. During the hymn or song before the sermon, I usually kneel down for a moment and pray. My prayer is nearly always something like this: "Lord, this is your Word, and these are your people, and I am only your spokesman for the next few minutes. Please make your Word come to life. Help me to be clear. Don't let me get lost. Keep me to time. Do your work, for your own glory, and for Christ's sake. Amen."

THE LAST SUPPER (MT 26:17-30)

The general context. When I was given this passage, I first of all read the whole chapter of Matthew 26. I noticed that while the second half dealt with the arrest and trial of Jesus, the first half was filled with different scenes of growing tension and danger in the two days immediately beforehand. So I wanted to help people to see that the scene of the Last Supper and the famous words of Jesus are set against a very dark and threatening background. And, particularly, I noticed that the account of that final meal of Jesus with his disciples is surrounded on both sides by sinful actions of his disciples: the plan by Judas to betray him (Mt 26:14-16) and the prediction that Peter will deny him (Mt 26:31-35). I think Matthew probably does this deliberately, showing that the death of Jesus (his body and blood) was for exactly this kind of sin. His own disciples were sinners like the rest of us, and Jesus knew it. We need to put ourselves in their place and understand our own need of forgiveness—which is what the whole story is about.

Explaining the Passover. Matthew's first readers would have known what happened every year in Jewish homes at Passover time with all the preparation that needed to be made and how the meal was arranged. And, since most of them would have been Jews, they would also have known from their Scriptures (our Old Testament) the significance of this annual event. But since many people today do not know these things, I felt it was important to spend a bit of time painting the picture for people, helping them to understand what was going on in the upper room, and why. By doing so, I hoped to get them engaged, in their imagination, with the scene itself as Matthew describes it.

In explaining the significance of the event in the second section of the sermon, I also had an eye on the end of my sermon, when I wanted to remind Christians that we too celebrate the great act of

God for our redemption, and to make the link between the Feast of Passover and our celebration of the cross of Christ when we partake in Holy Communion. So I was deliberately trying to increase the listeners' appreciation of the deep biblical meaning of that sacrament—something that can become just a regular part of a church's ritual, done without much understanding.

The words of Jesus. In Matthew 26:21-29, Jesus is the main speaker. As I studied the flow of what he said, it seemed to me that it falls into three sections:

- what he said about (and to) Judas, who betrayed him (vv. 21-25)

- what he said about the bread and wine, in relation to his own body and blood (vv. 26-28)

- what he said about the future joy of his Father's kingdom (v. 29)

So I broke it up into those sections and spent a little time on each of them. Naturally, I concentrated most on the so-called words of institution, meaning what Jesus said about the bread and wine. Since these words are so familiar to Christians who regularly go to Holy Communion, I wanted to set them in their original context in the middle of a Passover meal. I like to try to bring the Bible to life by engaging people's imagination, to help them be in the scene to see and hear what was going on. And I also wanted to show how the words about Jesus' blood echoed specific Old Testament texts that are very important for knowing how he meant his words to be understood. Once again, wherever one part of the Bible helps us to understand another, I think we should use that and help our listeners to see the connections. So this section of the sermon had a predominantly teaching purpose.

The conclusion. In the concluding section of the sermon, my aim was to help people see that coming to Communion is important for us. We should celebrate the historical event of the cross with as much joy and gratitude as the Israelites celebrated the exodus. It is all part of one great story—the biblical story of redemption, which includes Old and New Testaments.

I could have stopped there, but I felt I could not leave out the final little detail that was included in the passage I was given: "When they had sung a hymn, they went out to the Mount of Olives" (Mt 26:30). Again, many Christians today are unfamiliar with the Jewish Passover and the fact that, near the end, they recite a section of the book of Psalms known as the Great Hallel. It is almost certain that this would have been what Jesus and his disciples sang together as they left the meal and walked through and out of the city, knowing the danger Jesus was in from the authorities who wanted to arrest him.

So I turned to those psalms (Ps 113–118), and I read through them slowly, trying to imagine what it would have meant for Jesus himself to be saying or singing those words. What emotions filled his heart and mind? What prayers did he cry out to his Father? Well, we know what he prayed in the garden of Gethsemane, but he had already filled his mind with these words from the Psalms. And as I did that, several thoughts struck me, which I built into the final words of my sermon. It seemed to me that I was finishing the sermon in the same way that Matthew finishes his account of the Last Supper.

PETER'S DENIAL (MT 26:69-75)

Although the text I was given to preach from was the section of verses from Matthew 26:69-75, it seemed to me from the start of my preparation that this event was clearly important, given that it is described in all four Gospels in considerable detail. So I felt I should point that out and draw my preaching from different accounts as appropriate. I don't often do that. I think that when we preach from a specific Gospel passage we should try to focus on the distinctive emphasis of that Gospel writer himself. But on this occasion, I felt it was justified to make use of all the material, including John's Gospel, to give people the full flavor of an event that speaks very powerfully—spiritually and emotionally—still today.

Countering the cult of success. The second thing that I was very conscious of in my preparation was how our cultures (particularly in the West, but it is much more widespread) are success-oriented. We have made idols of success and celebrity. Sports heroes, TV and movie stars, the super-wealthy and famous—such people fill our media. And then there is all the pressure to succeed in business, in sex, in parenthood, in school, and at college. The stress caused by fear of failure starts very early in life and can be relentless. The idolizing of success can be terribly destructive and costly. False gods always are.

The same cultural idolatry can invade our spiritual lives too. We want to be "successful Christians." We want to be winners, not losers. We want to be seen to be "mightily used of the Lord," and so on. So the fear of failure—and the fact of failure—can be devastating.

So it seems to me that the story of Peter's terrible failure at the most critical moment in Jesus' life on earth is told at least partly to help all of us, disciples like Peter, to recognize the reality of failure, and to see how Jesus dealt with it in Peter's case. I wanted the sermon to be honest and truthful, to help people (myself as preacher as well as all who were listening) to face up to failure, and to experience the forgiving grace of God in a way that can only happen when we are actually honest enough to accept the truth in the presence of the Lord Jesus himself (as Peter had to).

Since the topic is very serious and the sermon would have some difficult and emotional sections, I decided to start with something more lighthearted. *The Book of Heroic Failures* provided that, and I used some early sections of it. But then I moved on from the funny side of failure to the fact that usually failure isn't funny at all, and from there moved straight to Peter.

Reliving the scene. I think it is always important with any narrative text (Old or New Testament) to help people get inside the story in their imagination, and feel it, not just read it. So in the first part of the sermon I tried to do that by pointing out some of the startling contrasts and ironies in the way the story is told. Peter's failure is surprising and shocking, and I wanted people to experience some of that emotion. As I went through the list of items in that part of the sermon, I referred to the relevant verses that illustrated each point. It was a way of immersing ourselves in the text itself and remembering the story in detail.

Facing facts. This was the part of the sermon where I wanted people to be honest and recognize that failure is part of real life, and that God knows it! So I stressed how the Bible is full of failures (which some people seem a bit surprised about, and yet it is obviously true). And I also wanted to preach against the success culture that can easily characterize a certain kind of Christian worship and church life. There are many people who have left churches because their own inner sense of failure could never match up to the constant celebration of great testimonies and miracles, or because there was no real pastoral attention to the realities of their lives.

Bringing Jesus into the picture. It struck me as remarkable that in all four Gospels, Jesus *predicts* Peter's denial. It is as if God wants to say, "You may be surprised that Peter failed, but I was not. Jesus knew." And that seems to be a major clue to the way the story leads to Peter's restoration. Surely there is a great relief in realizing that our sins and failures, even though of course they grieve our Lord, do not surprise him. He knows what we are. He knows our weakness. And he can cope with that!

So the final part of the sermon moved on to the way Peter was restored, both through Jesus' prayer and Jesus' probing. That is where I moved to John's account, which seems to show us that John witnessed both Peter's terrible denial and his remarkable restoration when he was able to tell Jesus that he loved him the same number of times as he had denied him.

So the story and the sermon end with failure forgiven. I do not usually end sermons with an altar call. But on this occasion I made the closing prayer (renamed "Reflection" for the purposes of this book) an opportunity for people to be open and honest in God's presence, confess their failure and weakness, and ask for God's forgiveness. This was not so much an evangelistic appeal as a moment for Christian believers to come back again into an honest and truthful relationship with God and to know his forgiveness.

INSULTS AND PARADISE (LK 23:26-43)

On this occasion I wanted to stay very close to Luke's own account, and try to bring out the unique way that he tells the story of the crucifixion. This sermon was part of a series in the weeks up to Easter in which different preachers preached on sections of Luke 22–24. So my sermon was just on the section from Luke 23:26-43.

Separating the scenes. I remember reading the passage again and again, trying to get inside it and discern what Luke was trying to convey through his mixture of description, quotation of Scripture, and the speeches of the characters.

The first thing I noticed was that Luke takes us through four scenes with four main sets of actors. If you read a text like this as if it were a movie script, you can notice when the camera angle changes and when you suddenly see a new character or a new scene. What is the movie director wanting you to see and hear as the scene changes? Here is what I saw and heard as I read through the narrative with that kind of imagination:

- the dialogue with the women on the way to the crucifixion
- the actions of the soldiers as they crucified Jesus
- the mockery of the bystanders and others
- the dialogue with the criminals on either side of Jesus

But in each case, I noticed that Luke, either explicitly or by intentional echoes and allusions, makes his readers remember Old Testament Scriptures that give meaning to each of the scenes; deeper meaning beyond the simple facts that we see with our eyes as we read the text. Luke is a very skillful author and writes in a way that even a child can understand. He simply tells the story of what happened during those terrible hours at Calvary. But he does so in such a way that those who know the Old Testament Scriptures can hear the significant references, and thus see beneath the surface of the mere facts.

So I decided to follow Luke's sequence and bring out those Old Testament Scriptures. I believe that it is usually good to make connections between the Old and the New Testament wherever it helps to deepen our understanding of the Bible as a whole, and this seemed a good opportunity to do it, since Luke seems to expect his readers to do so. So that's why I called them "four scenes full of Scripture."

Spotting the repetitions. The next thing I noticed was that Luke uses the same phrase three times:

- "let him save himself"
- "save yourself"
- "Save yourself and us!"

That kind of repetition can hardly be accidental. Luke is making a point. What is it? The point surely is that almost everybody around the cross was making fun of Jesus, urging him to save himself from the cross, but thinking, of course, that there was no way he could do so now that he was nailed to it. Yet, as Jesus had said when they came to arrest him, he could have called on battalions of angels to rescue him at any moment. He *could have* saved himself. But he chose not to do so. Luke is making it very clear that, in order to save us, Jesus *chose* not to save himself. Jesus chose to give up his life for us, and not to save himself from the cross.

So in my sermon, I made that point as strongly as I could. It was observing the repetition of the words that alerted me to it. When a biblical author repeats a word or phrase in the same passage, it is usually worth noticing and asking why. Just asking that question usually opens up some of the deeper significance of the passage that the author is wanting us to see.

Listening to Jesus. There are seven recorded sayings of Jesus from the cross, words he spoke after they had actually crucified him. Two of them come here in Luke's Gospel. So it seemed right to pull them out and highlight them in the sermon. One was his prayer for the soldiers: "Father, forgive them, for they do not know what they are doing" (Lk 23:34). The other was his promise to the repentant criminal, "Today you will be with me in paradise" (Lk 23:43). A prayer and a promise, and both of them remarkable and surprising. How should we understand them, and what do they teach us today?

So my sermon became a "four-three-two" structure; and I simply concluded by saying that it all led to one thing: the true meaning of Easter, as seen through the eyes of Luke.

FROM DARKNESS TO LIGHT (MK 15:33-39)

This was part of a sermon series on Mark's account of the cross and resurrection preached by several of the All Souls staff in the weeks up to Easter and during Holy Week. On this occasion I was given the section of Mark 15 that describes the actual crucifixion. So I focused on that alone and tried to discern how Mark wants us to see and understand the event.

Seeing a transition. Reading the passage again and again, I was struck with how it begins with a shock—darkness at midday! But then it ends with a kind of light going on in the mind of the Roman centurion, as he exclaims, "Surely this man was the Son of God!" (Mk 15:39), something that Mark has been wanting us to know and believe from the first verse of his Gospel. How amazing that it is a Roman soldier who has that moment of enlightenment, when others are still in the darkness of unbelief and mockery! So I decided to use that transition—from darkness to light—as the structure of the sermon as a whole.

Filling in the parts. Having decided on that structure, I then asked: What different kinds of darkness were involved in those three hours, both in nature itself and in the consciousness of Jesus? And, second, what kinds of light does Mark lead us into as he describes some of the things that happened as Jesus died? As you can read in the sermon, I felt there were four elements in each case.

In only one of those eight points did I feel that I was using some imagination or conjecture. On all the others I am confident that Mark would agree with the different points I make about the nature of the darkness and the dawning of the light of salvation. The one that is more of a guess is the first one under "Into the Darkness," where I suggest that part of the meaning of the darkness was that it hid Jesus from the glaring exposure to public shame that had been going on for three hours already. When the sun stopped shining, it took Jesus into the cover of darkness. It is probably going too far to suggest that that was the *purpose* of God darkening the sun, but it was certainly part of the *effect*. And I don't think I am wrong to imagine that when it turned dark the mockery of the people probably turned to awe and fear. So, as you read the sermon at that point, you may decide whether my interpretation is acceptable or too fanciful. Sometimes preaching treads a fine line between what is crystal clear in the text and what comes from using a little imagination on the text. We need to be careful not to stray too far into the second. I am willing to be told that maybe I did stray on this occasion; you can be the judge!

Probing the mystery. Mark records the most terrible of all the sayings of Jesus from the cross: "My God, my God, why have you forsaken me?" (Mk 15:34). Mark says that Jesus cried this at the climax of the hours of darkness. In any sermon about the cross it is surely vital to pay attention to the words Jesus spoke, and so I gave a large section of the sermon to exploring this cry.

At this point, I was very aware that people might easily be confused about what Jesus meant and what actually happened. Some people say it was just a subjective feeling of abandonment that Jesus experienced. But I believe it was much more than that, and that we need to try to understand the theological depths of the truth that Jesus did go through what our sin deserves; the separation from God his Father. We will never be able to understand fully what that meant, but I think it is important that we affirm it and know that it was for us. Jesus experienced it so that we will never need to, if we trust in him. So I gave a lot of time to explaining that as best I could.

I happen to like poetry and hymns! And many of the church family at All Souls are of a generation that appreciate them too. So I included a poem by Don Carson about that cry of Jesus. I found it appropriate since it also moves from darkness to light, even though, of course, I am well aware that it cannot translate into other languages.

Enjoying the light. Since it is well-known that that cry of Jesus comes from the first verse of Psalm 22, I thought it was important to say that probably Jesus would have had the whole psalm in his mind as he hung on the cross. And it is a psalm that moves from appalling agony and suffering in its first half to amazing praise and hope in the second half. So it is very likely that the "loud cry" that Mark describes as Jesus "breathed his last" (Mk 15:37) was the words that John 19:30 records: "It is finished," which echoes the last verse of Psalm 22, the victorious accomplishment of God that will bring joy and life to all creation. So I finished the sermon on a very positive note.

In my last section there is a point that I happily admit that I owe to one of the commentaries I read: the way Mark uses the verb "torn open" twice: for the tearing of heaven at the baptism of Jesus, and the tearing of the curtain in the temple at his death. In both cases a voice declares that Jesus is the Son of God. I think the commentary was right to say that Mark had done this quite deliberately, but I would not have noticed it by myself. However, having learned it from a commentary, it did seem significant enough to include in my sermon, since it serves to highlight what Mark himself wants us to see: that Jesus, the crucified Jesus, was and is the true Son of God.

IT IS FINISHED (JN 19:28-37)

I think that if I had planned a sermon series from John's account of the passion of Christ, I would have split this long passage into two sermons. There is enough in John 19:28-30 for one whole sermon. But I was given the whole passage of John 19:28-37, so I did my best to include it all!

Two viewpoints. As I read the text thoroughly I was struck by the personal note in John 19:35: "The man who saw it has given testimony . . ." These are the words of an eyewitness who was actually at the cross, John himself. He saw all that happened. So he is describing the event from his own point of view, and he tells us how one particular action, after Jesus had died, triggered memories of two Scriptures.

But then, as I read John 19:28-30, it seems that John is telling us what was going on in the mind of Jesus himself. As I say in the sermon, we can only assume that Jesus told John about this after the resurrection. And once again, it was the Scriptures that filled Jesus' mind and intentions in those moments before his death.

So, observing these different perspectives (what Jesus was thinking in John 19:28-30, and what John saw and remembered in John 19:31-37) led me to frame the sermon around those two angles. As mentioned before, it is sometimes helpful to imagine a biblical narrative as if it were a movie. What you see in a movie depends on the camera angle, and that depends on the director. So if the author of a biblical book is like the director of the movie, then the different scenes are like the different camera angles that he commands. You see everything from whatever point of view he provides for your eyes.

So that is how the sermon got its shape. John shows us the cross, first of all from within the mind of Jesus himself, and then through his own eyes as a witness who was standing there at the time. Even just framing the sermon like this seemed to bring the whole text to life (though I would still say it was too long as a single sermon, and I would prefer to split it into two if I were to preach this passage again).

What was Jesus thinking? As I studied John 19:28-30, listening to what John tells us Jesus was thinking and hearing what Jesus actually said, I was struck by how *purposeful* the whole passage is. John is not merely describing a crucifixion and telling us (what everybody would know anyway) that the man being crucified was terribly thirsty and they gave him a drink. Nor is he just telling us that Jesus simply died because he knew it was all over for him; he was "finished." No, he portrays these final moments of Jesus on the cross as a time of deliberate intention and great accomplishment. And that is surely surprising! How can a man who has been nailed to a cross, a man who is dying of thirst, a man who is at the very point of death—how can such a man be thinking of it all as something he has *achieved*? Yet that is what John tells us, by taking us into the mind of Jesus, as well as by recording for us two of the sayings of Jesus from the cross: "I am thirsty," and "It is finished."

A strong clue to all this becomes clear if you are able to read the text in Greek. Of course, for many preachers that is not possible. But even in translation, we should be able to feel the similarity between two of John's phrases: "everything had now been finished" (v. 28) and "It is finished" (v. 30). In Greek it is the same word. And the middle word, "would be fulfilled" (v. 28), is very similar, though not exactly the same. A good commentary ought to point this out.

In some churches there is a tradition of preaching the seven sayings of Jesus from the cross during Holy Week or on Good Friday itself. But usually, each saying is treated on its own and isolated from its context in the Gospel where it is recorded. I felt that, in preaching from this passage in John's Gospel, I needed to help people see how the two sayings John records ("I am thirsty" and "It is finished") are set within a passage in which Jesus speaks for a clear reason and purpose. The whole scene is one of fulfillment and accomplishment, and Jesus knew it and intended it. Those two saying were not just random exclamations; they were uttered with very clear intentions and achievements in mind. So in my sermon

I tried to explain the background Scriptures and to show how and why Psalm 22 especially (and as a whole) was shaping Jesus' thoughts and intentions at that moment.

Expanding the meaning of the cross. But I felt I needed to go a bit further. Another thing that happens in many churches is that the cross of Christ is preached in very personal terms: Jesus died to take your sin and my sin on himself, so that we might be forgiven. So, whether in an evangelistic appeal or as an encouragement and assurance to believers, we focus almost entirely on the salvation that God promises to each one of us personally and as individuals because Jesus died for us. Now, of course, that is all wonderfully true, and I believe it and rejoice in it! And in my sermon I did want to include that aspect.

But that idea (salvation for individual sinners) is not the sum total of what God accomplished through the cross of Christ. When Jesus cried out "It is finished"—or better, "It is accomplished"—what did he mean? He meant that he had accomplished all that God intended for the redemption of the world (including all creation) from evil, sin, and death. I felt it was important in my sermon to help people understand the full depth of what those words of Jesus actually meant.

So I made a short list of texts in the New Testament that speak about different dimensions of what God accomplished through the cross of Christ. He bore our guilt. He defeated the powers of Satan. He destroyed the power of death. He destroyed enmity and brought peace. He reconciled the whole creation to God. I did not go off on a tangent by explaining all these verses one by one (that would have made the sermon terribly long, and it would have strayed a long way from the passage in John's Gospel). I simply read each of them, pointing out that they were all part of the plan of God and therefore part of the accomplishment of Christ. What I was trying

to do at that point in the sermon was to broaden people's understanding and appreciation of what Jesus meant by "It is accomplished." I'm sure people would not immediately grasp each single
one that I mentioned, but I wanted the cumulative effect to hit
them. I wanted them to think, "Wow! The cross is *big*!"

It would be possible to follow up a sermon like this with a series
of group Bible studies on each of those passages that I quoted, all
of which speak of the cross in different ways. In the sermon itself
I just wanted to expand people's vision and arouse their amazement
and curiosity, hoping they might think, "I never realized there was
so much in what happened at the cross! I must go away and think
about that more deeply."

Teaching the atonement. Since the death of Jesus on the cross is
at the very heart of the gospel and the Christian faith, it is important that people do not have wrong ideas about it. One very
central way in which the Bible speaks about it is to see Jesus as our
substitute. Jesus took our place. It is our sin that deserves God's
judgment, but Jesus bore the wrath of God in our place. He carried
the consequences of our sin, even though he himself was sinless.
He took what we deserve, so that we can be forgiven.

However, some people speak and preach about this in a way that
can easily be misunderstood. They make it sound almost as if Jesus
was somehow separate from God. God should have punished us, but
he punished Jesus instead, as if Jesus were a third party, an innocent
victim who was forced to suffer what somebody else deserved. And
there are others who very much dislike that way of talking about the
atonement, saying that it makes God seem like a cruel father who
abuses his own son by punishing him for things he didn't do.

In my sermon I felt I should address this conflict of ideas by
emphasizing the way John describes the moment of Jesus' death:
"He bowed his head and gave up his spirit" (Jn 19:30). This makes

it clear that Jesus *chose* to die. He was not just killed, whether by the soldiers or by his Father. Jesus *willingly* gave himself up to die for us. The will of God the Father and the will of God the Son were entirely working together at the cross. God was not punishing somebody else instead of us. God was bearing all the cost and penalty of our sin *in his own self.* God took all the terrible consequences of sin and suffered for them himself in the person of God the Son. Or as Paul puts it, "God was reconciling the world to himself in Christ" (2 Cor 5:19). We should never place any division between the Father and the Son in the work of our salvation.

This is difficult to understand, of course. There is a lot of mystery even just trying to think about how the whole of God—the Holy Trinity—was involved in making atonement for our sin. But the Bible affirms it, and we should believe it. And preach it. So that is why I spent some time trying to explain that point and help people have a more biblical way of thinking about the cross.

Explaining the Scriptures. As I said, I would happily have finished my sermon at John 19:30, but I was given the rest of the passage down to verse 37. So, since it is the job of expository preaching to explain the Bible passage carefully, I needed to help people see what John himself saw, and how it made him remember two Bible texts from the Old Testament.

John saw that the Roman soldiers did not need to break Jesus' legs because he was already dead, and that one of them stabbed Jesus in the side, releasing a flow of blood and water. And the Old Testament passages that John recalled were from the Passover story (not a bone of the Passover lamb was to be broken, so John sees Jesus dying as the true Passover Lamb, saving people from judgment and death), and from Zechariah (where the people who had "pierced God" with their sin would mourn and repent of what they had done and find God's forgiveness and cleansing).

So I tried to explain these Bible quotations, and then, in my brief conclusion (the sermon had gone on long enough!), I summed up how John, in his description of the actual moments of Jesus' death, had taken us into the mind of Jesus (showing how the cross was actually God's great achievement), and had helped us to see what he saw, through the lens of the Bible texts he quoted.

ACKNOWLEDGMENTS

These chapters present each sermon more or less as it was preached. I am grateful to Vivian Doub for transcribing the audio recordings of the sermons with the help of my own handwritten notes. In preparing them for this book I have done only some necessary light editing from the transcripts. I am also grateful to All Souls Church for their permission to publish the sermons in this form. The original sermons may be accessed for listening free online through the All Souls website, allsouls.org.

NOTES

CHAPTER ONE: THE LAST SUPPER

13 *The Last Supper:* This sermon was preached at All Souls Church on March 2, 2008.

CHAPTER TWO: PETER'S DENIAL

33 *Peter's Denial:* This sermon was preached at All Souls Church on March 30, 2003.

33 *Success is overrated:* Stephen Pile, *The Book of Heroic Failures* (London: Routledge & Kegan Paul, 1979), 12.

34 *All four Gospels record:* Mt 26:31-35, 69-75; Mk 14:27-31, 68-72; Lk 22:31-34, 54-62; Jn 13:37-38; 18:15-27.

39 *Missionary Attrition:* William D. Taylor, ed., *Too Valuable to Lose: Exploring the Causes and Cures of Missionary Attrition* (Pasadena, CA: William Carey Library, 1997).

42 *An old hymn:* Joseph M. Scriven, "What a Friend We Have in Jesus," 1855.

48 *Bearing shame:* Philip Paul Bliss, "Man of Sorrows! What a Name," 1875.

CHAPTER THREE: INSULTS AND PARADISE

51 *Insults and Paradise:* This sermon was preached at All Souls Church on March 25, 2007.

68 *"I can't wish them evil":* Kathy Melvin, "Faiths unite to mourn the death of 21 Coptic Orthodox Christians," *Presbyterian News Service*, February 19, 2015, www.pcusa.org/news/2015/2/19/faiths-unite-mourn -death-21-coptic-orthodox-christ.

68 *"We don't forgive the act":* Daniel Burke, "Coptic Christian bishop: I forgive ISIS," *CNN*, February 20, 2015, www.cnn.com/2015/02/20/living /coptic-bishop-isis.

68 *Alan was a man:* Eleanor Harding, "As a Christian, I forgive my husband's two killers," *The Daily Mail*, July 18, 2013, www.dailymail.co.uk /news/article-2368574.

CHAPTER FOUR: FROM DARKNESS TO LIGHT

73 *From Darkness to Light:* This sermon was preached at All Souls Church on April 5, 2009.

80 *In the moment:* Donald Macleod, *A Faith to Live By* (Fearn, Tain: Christian Focus, 2002), 130-31.

83 *The darkness fought:* D. A. Carson, *Holy Sonnets of the Twentieth Century* (Grand Rapids: Baker Books; Nottingham, UK: Crossway Books, 1994), 51. Used by permission.

CHAPTER FIVE: IT IS FINISHED

89 *It Is Finished:* This sermon was preached at All Souls Church on March 20, 2005.

89 *"It is a far, far better thing":* Charles Dickens, *A Tale of Two Cities*, Bantam classic ed. (New York: Random House, 2003), 382.

98 *My sin, oh, the bliss:* Horatio Gates Spafford, "When Peace, Like a River, Attendeth My Way," 1873.

98 *It was my sin:* Stuart Townend, "How Deep the Father's Love for Us," Thankyou Music, 1995.

100 *We have no liberty:* John R. W. Stott, *The Cross of Christ*, 20th anniversary ed. (Downers Grove, IL: InterVarsity Press, 2006), 150-51.

103 *Let the water:* Augustus Toplady, "Rock of Ages," 1775.

104 *"full, perfect, and sufficient sacrifice":* From the liturgy of Holy Communion in the Anglican *Book of Common Prayer*.

106 *Every eye shall now:* Charles Wesley, "Lo! He Comes with Clouds Descending," 1758.

108 *He was lifted up:* Philip Paul Bliss, "Man of Sorrows! What a Name," 1875.

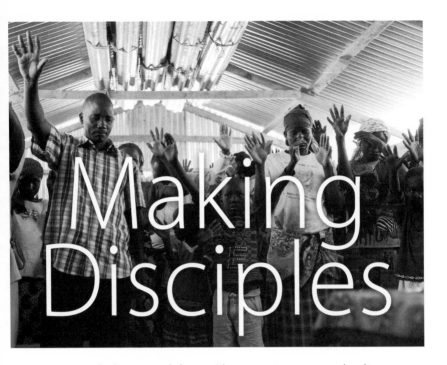

Making Disciples

Around the World — Christianity is exploding with growth in numbers

Yet — Believers are struggling to grow in Christ

That's Why Langham Exists

Our Vision

To see churches in the Majority World equipped for mission and growing to maturity in Christ through the ministry of pastors and leaders who believe, teach and live by the Word of God.

www.langham.org

FOUNDED BY JOHN STOTT
Langham®
PARTNERSHIP

ALSO BY
CHRISTOPHER J. H. WRIGHT

Knowing God the Father Through the Old Testament
Knowing Jesus Through the Old Testament (Second Edition)
Knowing the Holy Spirit Through the Old Testament

From the Bible Speaks Today Series:
The Message of Ezekiel
The Message of Jeremiah
The Message of Lamentations

Cultivating the Fruit of the Spirit: Growing in Christlikeness
The Mission of God: Unlocking the Bible's Grand Narrative
Old Testament Ethics for the People of God

All Chris Wright's royalties from this book have been irrevocably assigned to Langham Literature (formerly the Evangelical Literature Trust). Langham Literature is a program of the Langham Partnership International (LPI), founded by John Stott, where Chris Wright is the International Ministries Director. Langham Literature distributes evangelical books to pastors, theological students, and seminary libraries in the Majority World, and fosters the writing and publishing of Christian literature in many regional languages. For further information on Langham Literature and LPI, visit langham.org.